HOW TO IRON YOUR OWN DAMN SHIRT

ALSO BY CRAIG BORETH

The Hemingway Cookbook

HOW TO IRON YOUR OWN DAMN SHIRT

THE PERFECT HUSBAND HANDBOOK

FEATURING OVER 50 FOOLPROOF

WAYS TO WIN, WOO & WOW YOUR WIFE

CRAIG BORETH

ILLUSTRATIONS BY JAY MAZHAR

THREE RIVERS PRESS · NEW YORK

Published in the United States by Three Rivers Press, an imprint of the
Crown Publishing Group, a division of Random House, Inc., New York.
www.crownpublishing.com

THREE RIVERS PRESS and the Tugboat design are registered
trademarks of Random House, Inc.

Library of Congress Cataloging-in-Publication Data
Boreth, Craig.
    How to iron your own damn shirt : the perfect husband handbook featuring
over 50 foolproof ways to win, woo & wow your wife / Craig Boreth.—1st ed.
    Includes bibliographical references and index.
1. Husbands—Life skills guides.   2. Husbands—Humor.   3. Man-woman
relationships.   4. Men—Conduct of life.   I. Title.
    HQ756.B665   2005
    646.7'0086'55—dc22   2004025310

ISBN 1-4000-5362-5

Printed in the United States of America

Design by Lauren Dong

Illustrations by Jay Mazhar

10   9   8   7   6   5

First Edition

For Corinne, who knows perfection when she sees it

Acknowledgments

Thanks to everyone who helped make this book a success, including: super-agent Laurie Abkemeier, whose enthusiasm and support from day one made this book a reality; Jay Mazhar, who read through all my convoluted descriptions and created such excellent illustrations; Becky Cabaza, Orly Trieber, and everyone at Three Rivers Press; Gracia Walker and the good people at Kiehl's; Sammy Franco; Jack Chapman; Gay Courter; Charles Carlin; Tracy Smith; Beth Dart; Jeffrey Goldberg; Gary Lipshutz; Judy Krulewitz and Elizabeth Weinberger; Eric Reed; Katie Sharkey; Eric Yorkston for the battery-licking line; Sandy Green; Thomas Bahr; Tim Davis; Steve Weiss; Abby Gitlitz; Michael and Melissa Weiss; Mike Fuchs; Mike and Tori Palmer; Alyssa Ziman and Gary Weinhouse; Tom Pirone; Ira Frimere; Jill "Sarah" Connor; Andrew Ainslie; Sandrijn and Gary; Kate and Ernie Prudente; Jason Soslow; Margaret and Martin; Brad and Jenn; Fat Oscar; and, of course, Corinne.

Contents

SEX AND ROMANCE

AROUND THE HOUSE

IN THE KITCHEN

ON THE TOWN

HOW TO IRON YOUR OWN DAMN SHIRT

For Men Only

> *"Nobody made a greater mistake than he who did nothing because he could do only a little."*
>
> —EDMUND BURKE

All right, guys, settle down. I know some of you are pretty pissed off right now. You're probably sitting there thinking, "I've got a good thing going—I've convinced my wife to accept the minimal amount of husbandly diligence—and now this book comes along and ruins it all." Well, what if I told you that with just a little more effort, you could make her think that you're the kind of husband who actually does all those things she has long since come to accept that you just won't do? Imagine what you could get away with then.

The point is you'll never have to do everything in this book. But if you can master a few skills and learn to play a few mind games, you can reap the rewards of perfect husbandhood. And that's really the point. You don't have to be the perfect husband just for the sake of being perfect and pleasing your wife. It's really about just convincing her that you're the perfect husband and, consequently, pleasing you.

In order to make this arrangement work, you need to understand the mind of the wife and learn the rule of the game.

The Mind of the Wife

Women are complex, confusing, irrational, and downright dumbfounding. Married women doubly so. But their attitudes toward their husbands are pretty simple, if counterintuitive. There are three laws that govern the mind of the wife:

1. She doesn't expect you to always be perfect. Were you perfect when she married you? Hell, no. If she wanted perfection, she'd have dumped your sorry ass a long time ago.

2. She wants to form a *more perfect* husband. Nothing makes her happier than making you better. Keep in mind that just *thinking* she's made you better is good enough.

3. Perfection is in the eyes of her girlfriends (and her parents). Your wife doesn't necessarily need you to be perfect. She needs her girlfriends and her parents to think you're perfect, and then tell her so as soon as you leave the room.

The Rule of the Game

Many men treat their marriage like what's known as a "zero-sum game." You win, she loses, and the net result is zero. Of course, a marriage built on lots of zero-sum games doesn't add up to much. You don't want to approach your marriage like a battle, but rather like a negotiation, where each party comes away feeling good about the outcome. In other words, you want to win the battle of the sexes by convincing your wife that, in reality, she has won. That's what this book is all about.

In closing, let me just leave you with a bit of advice that you should carry forth as you embark on your journey toward perfect husbandhood. If you remember one thing from this book, it should be this single guiding principle, this cardinal law, above all other laws: Foreplay matters.

Go in peace, my brothers.

For Women Only

"Nothing so needs reforming as other people's habits."
—Mark Twain

All right, ladies, listen up. You're probably sitting there, grinning like the Cheshire Cat, figuring you've found your ticket to a life of leisure, lying supine and groggy, fanned with palm fronds and fed overripe figs, dispatching him with a wave of your hand to the kitchen and the dirty dishes. Well, remember those classic whodunits, when they'd haul away the evil genius, and someone would say, "If only he'd used his powers for good, instead of evil." Well, ladies, you've got a choice to make.

If you hang this book, like the sword of Damocles, above your husband's head, he'll wilt under the pressure (quite literally, if you catch my drift). You must let him find his own way on the path to perfection, and you must reward his efforts along the way.

Responsible use of this book is governed by three guidelines:

1. If you're worried about giving your husband this book, you should be. In other words, the more your husband needs this book, the less likely he is to read it, especially if he gets it from you. If this is the case, buy the book yourself, but give it to his brother (or better yet, his mother) to deliver.

2. Don't ever let him see you reading it. If you thought he wouldn't follow orders before, just wait until he sees you flipping through it. After that, any request you make will be tainted,

leaving him feeling so suspicious and manipulated, he'll question your motives when you ask him to pass the butter.

3. Reward his efforts. This book includes a lot of step-by-step instructions for how to do things. It also includes tricks to convince you he's seen the light. Either way, you're better off. So play along, let him feel he is winning. The net result will be a more perfect husband.

Given the proper motivation and reinforcement, your perfect husband will emerge, but it takes time. You must accept and appreciate each moment of perfection when you find it, with a cleaned kitchen here and a toilet seat put down there. You see, perfect husbandhood is a journey, not a destination. And as with all journeys, you know he'll never ask for directions, so this book is the only chance you've got.

Good luck, ladies.

THE MALE MIND
AND BODY

How to Know Your Limitations

*"Relax, all right. My old man is a television repairman,
he's got this ultimate set of tools. I can fix it."*
—JEFF SPICOLI (SEAN PENN),
Fast Times at Ridgemont High

"Man's got to know his limitations."
—HARRY CALLAHAN (CLINT EASTWOOD),
Magnum Force

This book is filled with instructions for things you need to know in order to be the perfect husband. But to start things off, let's take a moment to figure out how to know when *not* to do something. You're faced with a task that you figure is pretty straightforward. Your wife, of course, is skeptical, and happy to let you know it. Do you take a stand, or fold like a cheap map? Sometimes (not nearly as often as your wife would prefer, of course) a real man must admit he's completely clueless and defer to wiser minds. The question is, how do you know when to go with your gut, dive right in, and let the chips fall where they may, and when to take the mature (i.e., whipped), sensible (i.e., uninspired), and responsible (i.e., boring) path?

The two questions you must ask yourself are:

1. How difficult is this task?
2. What are the consequences if I screw it up?

You must take each factor into consideration when deciding how to proceed. For example, replacing the air filter in your home's central air-conditioning unit might be a simple maneuver. But if your in-laws are arriving tomorrow for Labor Day weekend, you'd better get a professional in there to guarantee it's done right.

The difficulty of a task is basically defined by your own familiarity with it, the accessibility of instructions for how to do it, and the number of special tools involved. If you're pretty sure you know where the air filter goes, and the guy down at Sears can get you the right filter, and all you need is a screwdriver, you're all set. But if you don't know the first thing about a project, don't have any idea where to look for help, and have never even heard of an immersion heater spanner, forget about it.

This brings us to the three areas of disastrous consequence to consider:

1. Exorbitant cost
2. Familial ridicule
3. Bodily harm

If you try to replace your car's timing belt and screw it up, you're probably in for a new engine. If you crash the aforementioned air-conditioning, you've got a weekend of sweaty in-laws ahead of you, and if you plan a best-of-seven hoops grudge match with your old college roommates, you'll likely end up hospitalized (or worse). So, here are some guidelines to help you know your limitations:

Ironically, the best way to know your limitations is to never find out what they are. That is, never get close enough to see the light at the end of the tunnel, which invariably will be the anemic fluorescent glow from a hospital room or lawyer's office. So, be honest with yourself. If you've got bad mojo around car engines, electricity, or black diamond trails, then just don't go there.

If you're seriously considering taking on a new task, follow this rule: If in doubt, hire it out. That means if *you* are in doubt, not if your wife is in doubt. She's not yet convinced you can gargle without choking each morning, let alone change the oil or carve a turkey. The key is how you honestly feel about your abilities. If you're really not sure, then hire a professional the first time (for the turkey carving, that means defer to her father), learn how it's done, and consider doing it yourself next time. If you're certain you can do it, there are still some steps to take to ensure that you actually can.

If you're about to embark on a project you've never done before, you've got to get your hands on authoritative instructions. That means finding a book on the subject (preferably the one you're holding in your hands right now), or a friend who knows what he's doing, or both. The book will tell you how it's done, the friend will tell you if it's possible. And all throughout this process, don't forget to always consider (1) how difficult this undertaking is and (2) what the consequences are. If, after conducting proper research and determining that both the difficulty and consequences are reasonable, only then may you proceed. Otherwise, get professional help.

See "How to Be Handy" (page 96) for some suggestions to help you do the job right. The most important tip is "Use the Correct Tool for the Job." Nothing will accentuate your ineptitude like hammering nails with a monkey wrench or scraping off putty with a kitchen knife. If you're stuck on a job because you can't jury-rig a tile cutter from a circular saw, two pizza boxes, and a garden hose, then you've reached your limit. Go out and buy the right tool, and get the job done. But even then you may want to take a moment to make sure your insurance is up to date.

One final thought: Another way to help you determine whether or not to charge forth with a particular endeavor is to think about how your obituary would read if things didn't work out quite so well. "Tragic spackling accident" is no way for a real man to go.

How to Get a Close Shave

A recent study by a British aftershave maker found that 92 percent of women prefer a clean-shaven man. The study also found that 63 percent of men believe that facial hair makes men more attractive. These results suggest an intriguing connubial conundrum. She wants him to shave off the mustache or, more likely, the goatee that he's had since college (or his most recent midlife crisis). He'd rather not, believing that his facial hair is a babe magnet.

She has two options: Force him to shave, and risk him shacking up with a gaggle of nubile young coeds. Or leave him hairy, and rest assured that no young chippie is going to come along and steal him away. Given that the odds of the former scenario occurring are zero on a good day, I'm guessing she'll take her chances with a clean-shaven husband.

Salvation for the hirsute hubby lies in his learning how to get the smoothest shave with the least irritation, chafing, and blood loss.

Getting a close shave is actually quite easy, but for some reason men have been misinformed over the generations and have suffered needlessly. Actually, since we're incapable of asking for help, just like our fathers and their fathers before them, we're pretty much using the same technique employed by our great-great-grandfathers back in the old shtetl in Minsk. It's time to update things a bit.

First of all, modernizing does not necessarily mean new

technology. I've never known those electric shavers to work. They look pretty good in the commercials, but as I'm told, commercials are not the most accurate reflection of reality (who knew?). So, get your hands on a good disposable razor, with at least two blades. I'm partial to the Gillette Sensor, but I'll use whatever higher-end razor they've got at Costco that day.

Now, next time your wife drags you to one of those big department stores, head straight for the men's grooming section. Tell them you want a good shave cream and aftershave (and, if you really want to take the plunge, invest in a badger-hair brush, and then buy shave cream designed for use with it). Specialty brands like Kiehl's (www.kiehls.com) will make all the difference over the products you've been using, by taking care of your skin and setting you up for a great shave.

Timing is the key to a close shave. You always want to shave *after* you shower. The steam and hot water from the shower will open up your pores and soften your beard. When you get out of the shower, crank up the hot water in the sink, as hot as you can stand it. If you've ever wondered why anyone would ever need a washcloth, here's your answer: Soak that sucker with hot water, apply it to your face, and hold it there for a few seconds. Before applying the shave cream, you may want to try using a facial scrub to exfoliate your skin. Kiehl's sells a Pineapple Papaya Facial Scrub that works wonders.

Next apply the shave cream. Forget about those foams and gels you've been using. It's time to get a real cream that you apply by hand or with a brush. If you've got sensitive skin, be sure to use a cream with mint or chamomile to soothe your skin. Kiehl's Green Eagle Shave Cream works great. Forget about lathering up; all you want is a barely visible film, enough to protect your face but not clog up your razor. Using your fingertips or a shaving brush, massage the shave cream into your beard in tight, circular motions, starting with an upward motion (against the grain). When you're done, get the hot water running again, wash off your hands, place your razor in the sink, and cover it with hot water. This gives you a little time to admire your manly physique before the metal meets the mug.

Start your shave with the least sensitive parts of your face, usually the cheeks. Use smooth, steady downward strokes, rinsing the razor thoroughly after every few strokes. For most men, the neck is the most sensitive part, so we'll leave that for last and do the chin and upper lip next. This gives the moisturizer in the shave cream the maximum possible time to soften up your beard. When you get to the neck, keep in mind that you want to keep shaving with the grain, which in some cases may not be downward but sort of sideways toward your throat. Just follow the grain on your face and you'll be all right.

When you're done, check for any missed spots (especially along the jawline), then rinse your face with warm water and pat dry with a towel (don't wipe your face—it can irritate freshly shaven skin). Then apply just a little bit of alcohol-free moisturizing aftershave.

There you go, nothing but smooth shaving from now on. And, by the way, about those nubile young coeds? It ain't gonna happen, beard or no beard, so get over it.

How to Eliminate Gas

Difficulty

T T T

Reward

♥ ♥

Like peeing in the shower or testing a nine-volt battery on your tongue, recognizing the intrinsic humor in flatulence clearly distinguishes men from women. From SBDs to Dutch ovens, we have created our own little stinky ecosystem around our love of farting. And yet, since women still refuse to recognize the humor in it, the perfection-seeking husband must find a way to tame his boisterous bowels.

There are many things a man can do to stifle his nether wind. None of these solutions are permanent, so if you've got a fishing weekend with the boys coming up, rest assured that you can easily fire up the big guns again with just a flew slices of pepperoni pizza and a six-pack.

First, identify foods that give you the most gas, and avoid them. Most likely offenders include beans, broccoli, onions, spicy food, dairy products, high-fiber foods, ice cream, soda, and beer. Except for the beer, you can probably live without most of those. But unfortunately, fried foods and fatty foods are also on the list. And, no, fried fatty foods don't somehow cancel each other out and make both acceptable. Nice try, though. You may want to try eliminating one food at a time, and see if that makes a difference. It may just be that only one or two foods bring the vapors, and everything else is fine.

Next, address the way you eat. Try eating five or six small meals throughout the day, rather than two or three huge meals. Just be careful that you don't end up eating five or six huge meals. While you're eating, be sure to eat slowly, take small bites, and chew your food thoroughly. Try to relax when you're eating, and avoid eating meals in your car or on the run. Also, eating with your mouth open or talking while you eat increases your chances of getting gas. Finally, try a cup of peppermint tea at the end of a meal; it can calm your digestion. At this point, all you'd have to do is extend your pinky while sipping your tea to become the veritable Eliza Doolittle of perfect husbands.

If you're still not having any luck, you can try an antigas product such as Beano, which must be taken with your first bite of food, or other products like Lactaid, to help with lactose digestion, or acidophilus, to replenish beneficial digestive bacteria.

If all else fails, you can try Under-Ease antiflatulence underwear, which filters out the unpleasant smell of "bad human gas (malodorous flatus)." According to their website (www. under-tec.com), Under-Ease is a "revolutionary new underwear for offensive gas" from "the leader in odor suppressant technology for flatulence." Can't argue with that!

I realize that with each stifled fart the world becomes a slightly less happy place, and in these troubled times we need all the laughter we can get. But that's the price of perfection.

How to Get Six-Pack Abs

Difficulty
_T T T T_

Reward
♥ ♥ ♥ ♥

Our hotshot team of nutritionists and physical therapists here at Perfect Husband Laboratories recently completed a study calculating a husband's chances of ever getting six-pack abs. Their findings are illustrated in the chart below:

AGE	YOUR CHANCES
<30	Slim
>30	None

Now wait a second, wasn't the whole purpose of getting married that you wouldn't have to stay in shape anymore? Seriously, how many women have dumped their husbands because he let himself go? Well, quite a few actually, so maybe that's not the best example. The fact is, in addition to everything else, the perfect husband should have washboard abs as well. So let's forget for the moment that it'll never happen, and figure out a way to use that unattainable goal to your advantage.

Keeping in mind that perfect husbandhood is a journey and not a destination, let's make the most of your attempt at abdominal improvement. First of all, don't keep it a secret. Make sure your wife and all her friends know you've decided it's time to get washboard abs. In fact, why not make it a birthday present for your wife (of course, tell her this as soon after her most recent birthday as possible, giving you the maximum time for improvement, and to soak her appreciation for all it's worth).

The biggest obstacle to real improvement in the abs is that it takes so long to see any results. You change your diet and start doing sit-ups, and after three weeks nothing has changed. Why even bother? So, here are a few things you can do to at least create the illusion of progress more quickly.

First, dress to slenderize. Remember, vertical lines make you look thinner. Also, try wearing darker colors, particularly dark pants with a lighter shirt, and maybe even matching dark-colored shirt and pants. Finally, try flat-front pants instead of pleats. And unless you're in a wedding party that absolutely requires it, don't ever wear a vest.

The easiest way to actually reduce your gut is to stand up straight. You'll be amazed at how much better you'll look and feel when you improve your posture. This is something that will take a little time and practice to maintain, but it's not nearly as difficult as all those crunches.

Next, let's tweak your diet a bit. Or, tweak it a lot. Actually, perhaps you should just stop eating altogether. Maybe that's a bit drastic. Let's try to come up with something more reasonable. Rather than overwhelm you with some complicated diet regimen, let's just go over some of the basic rules for a healthy diet. These guidelines build the foundation for good eating habits, and you should work to make them part of your lifestyle. If you want to embark on a more elaborate diet, consult your doctor, trainer, or a dietitian for a program customized for you.

1. Cut back on red meat. I'm not talking all tofu all the time, but try eating more chicken and fish, and less beef.

2. Cut back your intake of refined sugar and white flour.

3. Cut out fast food and fried foods completely. This one may be tough, but you're just going to have to do it if you want better abs.

4. Cut back on the booze. I would never recommend that a married man stay sober all the time, but just try drinking less.

5. Eat more home-cooked meals. Don't rely on your wife, do it yourself. This way, you can control the ingredients and portion sizes. Use fresh vegetables and olive oil for a particularly healthy and delicious meal. (See "How to Make a Stir-Fry," page 174, for additional suggestions.)

6. Rather than two or three big meals a day, try eating five or six small meals. Eat slowly, chewing your food completely, and be sure to drink plenty of water during meals and throughout the day.

7. If you get hungry during the day, keep healthy snacks on hand. Try a banana, an apple, or an energy bar like PowerBars or Clif Bars. Or, have a few tablespoons of peanut butter. It's delicious, it fills you up quickly, and all that fat is monounsaturated (the same "good fat" as in olive oil) and can actually help you lose weight.

Finally, you've got to exercise, to help reduce your body fat and increase your muscle mass. Ideally, you'll want to do some type of aerobic exercise for at least thirty minutes, three to five times a week. And, no, fidgeting while you're waiting for the next batch of fries at McDonald's does not count as aerobic exercise. So, get on a bike, a treadmill, or whatever. Just get moving.

You'll also want to get into a regular weight-training regimen. Increasing your lean muscle mass actually helps promote your metabolic rate, so you'll burn more calories, even while you're sitting on the couch watching football. You'll want to get the most out of your workout and avoid injuries, so be sure to consult with a personal trainer who can set you up with the proper workout for you. And remember, any exercise is better than none.

Finally, we come to the bane of man's existence: the abdominal workout. I'm convinced the human male has some genetic predisposition to despise sit-ups and crunches. To minimize the anguish, our plan is to do only five to ten minutes of ab work every day. It helps if you concentrate less on the "every day" part and more on the "five to ten minutes" part. To maximize the results, we're going to focus on only those exercises that work the abdominal muscles most effectively.

A few years ago, researchers at the biomechanics lab at San Diego State University studied thirteen different abdominal exercises to determine which were the most effective. Subjects engaged in each of the exercises to determine the levels of electrical activity each one stimulated in the two main abdominal muscle groups. The best four exercises were "the Bicycle Maneuver," "the Captain's Chair," crunches on an exercise ball, and vertical leg crunches.

The Bicycle Maneuver

Lie on your back with your hands at the sides of your head (fingers laced behind or with your fingertips gently behind your

ears). Bring your shoulder blades up off the ground and move your legs in a cycling motion, touching your left elbow to your right knee and then your right elbow to your left knee. Keep a slow, steady pace and keep breathing regularly. Start with three sets of ten to twenty-five repetitions, and increase from there.

The Exercise Ball

This exercise also requires a piece of equipment, but it's cheap enough to buy for use at home. This exercise was determined by researchers to be the best overall, since it required less work by the hip flexors and was the most efficient. Sit on the ball with your feet on the floor. Roll yourself forward until your thighs and torso are horizontal (at this point you'll know if the ball is too big or too small for you). Cross your arms on your chest and, as you exhale, raise your torso up to a forty-five-degree angle, contracting your abdominals. Hold this position for a moment, and then slowly lower yourself back to horizontal while you inhale.

The Captain's Chair

This exercise requires an apparatus found in most gyms. It's a simple, tall structure with two horizontal armrests and a vertical back support. You step up into it backward, supporting yourself on your forearms and elbows with your legs dangling. Slowly bring your knees up to your chest, focusing on your abdominal muscles, and then slowly lower your knees back down. A more difficult variation involves leaving your legs straight and raising your feet out in front of you until they're parallel to the floor.

The Vertical Leg Crunch

Lie flat on your back with your hands behind your head, fingers laced. Cross your legs at the ankles and raise them as close to vertical as you can, keeping your knees slightly bent. As you exhale, contract your abdominals and raise your torso up toward your knees, keeping your chin away from your chest. Hold this position for a moment, and then slowly come back down as you inhale. Keep your shoulder blades off the ground throughout, to prevent your abs from resting in between reps.

So, that's all there is to it. Just improve your diet, get sweating, lift some weights, and work those abs. The most important part of this whole process is to incorporate all this into your lifestyle, and make a healthy habit of it. Stick to it, and over time you'll see an improvement. And, more important, your wife will, too.

How to Stop Snoring

When I was in college, the guy in the room next to mine snored so loudly that the wall in between acted like a giant woofer and actually amplified the sound into my room. Each night I'd be jarred into semiconsciousness by the clamor, awakened from my recurring dream of bedding Tawny Kitaen atop an apple-red Jaguar parked in an elephant seal rookery.

If you're a snorer, your wife is either lucky enough to be able to sleep through the din, or she's strong-willed enough to keep herself from going Cuckoo's Nest on you with a pillow every night. Do your wife a favor—hell, do the neighbors a favor—and do whatever it takes to stop that infernal racket.

First of all, don't be one of those snorers who denies that he snores. What possible motivation could your wife have to lie about something like that? She's got plenty of real things to nag you about. There's no need to make up items to add to the list. If she says you snore, then you snore. The best way to start solving the problem is to tell her to shove you over on your side whenever you're snoring. She shouldn't hesitate at all to give you a sharp jab to the solar plexus whenever the snoring begins.

Along those same lines, you should try to sleep on your side, or at least try turning your head if you sleep on your back. Since snoring is often caused by the sagging of the throat muscles when they relax, you may want to try propping up your head a bit higher to mitigate the effects of gravity. (By the way, astronauts don't snore, since gravity doesn't exist in space.)

Drinking can cause further relaxation and inflammation of these muscles, which is why we often snore when sleeping off an all-night bender. You may also be more prone to snoring if you're overweight, so try and trim down a bit and see if that helps. You should also know that eating before bed can cause snoring, but following a good diet should keep you from eating late at night. And, of course, smoking can only make things worse, so here's yet another good reason to quit.

If none of these things helps, consult your doctor. You may have a potentially dangerous condition called sleep apnea, which can cause you to stop breathing for several seconds throughout the night. Or you may have a chronic sinus condition that exacerbates the problem. Regardless, your doctor should be able provide any number of medications, devices, and other possible solutions.

How to Have a Reasonable Midlife Crisis

Typical midlife crises fall into one of two categories, what David Brooks in *The Atlantic Monthly* called "the sensitive New Age spiritual quest and the vulgar materialist binge." The former is usually the more manageable, unless you end up selling the house, the car, and the kids on eBay and relocating permanently to a yurt in Myanmar. The latter is where you're more likely to get yourself in real trouble. Brooks wistfully describes this type of midlife crisis as making "the men around you privately envious and sensible women publicly retch." Unfortunately, your wife is one of those sensible women, so if you find yourself down at the local BMW dealership looking for something in a little red coupe, or at a local nightclub looking for someone in a little red dress, you need to take a moment and make sure you're not about to do something really stupid or, worse yet, something that will get the lawyers involved.

There are as many reasons for midlife crises as there are men who experience them. Some men feel that their lives have been empty, worthless ventures; they see the end approaching and feel they have nothing to show for it. Some may regret chances not taken, and feel they've been living a lie. Still others may be experiencing hormonal changes that affect them physically and mentally. The one thing the experts agree on is that this "crisis" is really just a change. It's not the end of the world, but a transition to a new one, and you want the people and things that are truly important to you to be there when you settle on the other side. Granted, it's a big change, but it's one that can be embraced and dealt with positively, helping you to appreciate your life in its entirety and allowing you to move forward with your self-esteem, and your marriage, intact.

Gay Courter, coauthor of *How to Survive Your Husband's Midlife Crisis*, offers these suggestions to help you make the most of your midlife change:

1. Take care of yourself. Exercise can work wonders for your mood and help you look better at the same time. Get a medical checkup and make sure everything's working right. If you and your wife are having sexual problems, recognize that there are lots of options to help you out (this is the age of Viagra, after all). Don't let these manageable issues become major problems.

2. If you're feeling irritable and angry more often than usual, or if your self-esteem is often low, you may be experiencing depression. Also, if you're drinking more or taking drugs, you may be trying to self-medicate to alleviate the symptoms. (I don't need to tell you about the folly of using depressants to alleviate depression.) Men are notoriously bad at seeking help for depression, but there's no reason not to. Psychotherapy can help, and there are many excellent antidepressants that can level out your mood. Basically, is just comes down to asking yourself why you should feel like crap if you don't have to.

3. Rather than using this "crisis" as an opportunity to indulge yourself with material things and false emblems of youth, try serving others. Courter recommends volunteering for causes important to you or becoming a mentor. These activities will remind you that your positive mark on this world does matter and does make a difference.

4. Take this opportunity to expand your horizons, and take some of those risks you may regret having avoided in the past. Just approach them sanely, and remember that this is not an end but a beginning, so plan accordingly. Learn to hang glide or go skydiving. If you've always dreamed of changing careers,

and can afford to take the risk, go for it. Take some time to travel. Whisk your wife away to Tuscany and Venice. If you go alone, be sure to get a round-trip ticket.

5. Finally, in addition to these other strategies, don't discount the benefit of getting that little red sports car or having cosmetic surgery to make yourself feel better. The key is to approach these things responsibly. Don't break the bank on a car you can't afford, and don't expect miracles from a little tummy tuck. Talk these things through with your wife—after all, she may need that little red sports car just as much as you do. (If you can get her to budge on the "little red dress" scenario, then you truly are entering your golden years.)

COMMUNICATION

How to Listen

The average husband hears about the first five words of anything his wife says before she begins to sound like the schoolteacher in those old Charlie Brown cartoons. Shortly thereafter, he regresses into a fidgety, hand-wringing, jingle-humming mess. My guess is that most men would actually like to be able to listen, but it's just not something that comes naturally. The male mind is transfixed by football, belly shirts, and pizza. How can anything a wife has to say possibly compete with that?

Salvation for the terminally distracted lies in a very simple technique used by teachers, therapists, and mediators called "active listening." If you use these techniques while she's telling you about what's-her-name's boyfriend and how he won't commit, and how she can't find pants that fit, and how you still need to clean up the garage, and wuh whaah wuh whah whahhhhhh. . . . Sorry, spaced out there for a second. Just try active listening. It works.

There are three main components to active listening: body language, asking questions, and summarizing.

Body Language

Ever wonder why your wife gets upset when you sit there "listening" to her with your arms and legs crossed, facing away from her and staring at the wall? It's because your body is screaming out that you'd rather be doing absolutely anything other than sitting there listening to her. Use your body to show her that you're paying attention:

- Stop whatever you're doing: Put down your beer, the sports section, whatever, and actually lean slightly toward her.
- Make eye contact: Try to maintain it for about 80 percent of the time.
- Open up: Uncross your legs and arms, and sit in a relaxed posture.
- Acknowledge: Nod your head in agreement, or furrow your brow with empathy.
- Give a few "uh-huh"s to let her know you're still with her. Be careful not to start nodding like a bobble head, or she'll know you've drifted off again, starring in that beer commercial in your mind.

Ask Questions

Asking questions is the easiest way to show that you're listening, and that you actually care about what she's saying. Ask open-ended questions to elicit more information. For example, ask "How did you feel about that?" or "Could you give me an example of what you mean?" Avoid questions that will put her on the defensive, such as "What the hell were you thinking?"

Summarize

This is a more advanced technique that requires some practice to master. It involves collecting the main points and expressing them back to her. You'll start a summary with "So, if I understand what you're saying . . ." or "Am I right that you're point is . . ." The risk here is that you'll talk over her, which is almost as bad as not listening in the first place. Be patient, let her finish what she has to say, and wait for a chance to summarize.

Remember, you don't have to really care about anything she's saying, but if you open up, acknowledge, ask questions, and summarize, she'll think you do. And that's all that really matters. Finally, keep in mind that all of this will help you with that other related skill she'd like to see some improvement on: "How to Remember What the Hell She Said Just Yesterday."

How to Talk About Your Feelings

Difficulty
T T T T
Reward
♥ ♥ ♥

"A new mood is in the air in Springfield, as refreshing as a premoistened towelette. Folks are finally accepting their feelings, and really communicating with no holding back, and this reporter thinks it's about [bleep]ing time."
—KENT BROCKMAN, *"The Simpsons"*

It's not that we don't want to talk about our feelings. Well, it's not *just* that. Family therapist Michael Gurian believes men are biologically predisposed to silence in stressful situations. His book *What Could He Be Thinking? How a Man's Mind Really Works* includes a list of ten ways our brains differ from those of women, including biological and hormonal differences that he believes explain why women love to talk about their feelings and men don't. Gurian may be on to something, and I'm sure most guys are happy to blame it all on their brain stems, but I believe much of the time we're just completely clueless about what our feelings actually are. If we can't tell ourselves what's going on, we sure won't be able to tell the wife. So, when she asks us what's wrong and we say "nothing," it's not technically a lie. But as I'm sure you already know, your wife long ago stopped accepting ignorance as an excuse. Sooner or later you're going to have to do better.

The first thing we'll do is help you figure out what you're feeling, and then we'll work on the best way to express those feelings.

Before we get started, let me clarify that the feelings we're talking about here are those embarrassing ones you've been taught to keep buried way down deep inside since you were a kid. Sure, you're aware of the profound sense of joy inspired by cold beer, hot wings, or that Pam Anderson–Tommy Lee home video, but those are not exactly the feelings your wife is longing for you to share. She wants to know about your fears and frustrations (also, jealousy and insecurity—just not when they're inspired by the Pam Anderson video). You know, the girly stuff.

There are a couple of ways we can begin to get in touch with our feelings. One is to think back on moments when you were angry or sad or frustrated. If your wife dragged you to see *Bridget Jones's Diary*, you probably felt all three. Another strategy would be to focus on your own emotions moving forward. If you're having a tough day at work or you're playing a miserable round of golf, take a moment to ask yourself a few questions:

1. What is this emotion I'm feeling?
2. Why am I feeling this way?
3. What, if anything, can I do about it?

Recognize that it's okay to feel this way. As you begin to get comfortable with acknowledging your own emotions, eventually you can begin to ask these questions out loud (try talking out loud while looking in the mirror). Eventually, you'll find that when your wife asks you what's wrong, you'll have an acceptable answer for her.

The Power of "Because"

The next challenge is to give her a satisfactory answer. If you finally take the huge step of telling her you're frustrated or depressed or scared, but then clam up when she asks you why, you're only halfway there. What you really need to do is complete this statement:

I feel [name emotion] because [explain reason for emotion].

A great way to learn how to talk about your feelings to her satisfaction is to listen to how she talks about her feelings (see "How to Listen," page 29). She'll give you more details than you ever wanted to know, but that means she expects the same in return.

Don't worry, you won't need to open up completely right away, sitting up all night gabbing, eating Nutter Butters and wearing your jammies and those fuzzy pink slippers (no matter how comfortable they may be). She's been so starved for emotional nourishment from you that she could OD if you give her too much at once. Dole it out in dribs and drabs—a little sadness here, a bit of frustration there. If you ration your emotions correctly, you won't need to shed a tear for years.

How to Apologize Convincingly

Difficulty

T T

Reward

♥ ♥ ♥ ♥

The initial step in apologizing convincingly is, first and foremost, to know what it is you're apologizing for. Your wife has mad Grizzly Adams skills when it comes to setting traps for you, and this one is her double-barreled ball-buster. First she gets you to apologize, and just when you think you're free and clear, she finds out you have no idea what you did wrong, and suddenly you're worse off than when you started. Remember the cardinal rule of confessions: Apologizing for unknown offenses is worse than not apologizing at all.

So, you have two possible scenarios when facing an imminent apology: one in which you're not aware of the offense, and one in which you are.

Clueless Joe

She's demanding an apology, and you have no idea what you've done. This is a situation fraught with peril. You know you can't apologize blind (see above), so you've got to figure out what you did wrong.

Do not guess. It's not worth the risk of telling her about something she didn't know about and digging the hole even deeper. Luckily, you've got a brief window of time between when you sense something's wrong and when the cowering begins. The first thing to do is get in touch with her best friend. Your wife has no doubt talked to her, and they've both agreed that she should be royally pissed. The best friend will probably tell you what you've done, and by the time your wife finds out that her friend bailed you out, the worst will already by over.

If you can't track down her best friend, you'll have to read her clues and let her lead you to the offense like a puppy to a soiled rug. First, look around for any evidence she has collected. A credit-card statement would indicate that she knows about the $500 you charged at Club Paradise in Vegas, or the greens fees from the weekend you were supposedly visiting your parents. If she just bought tickets for a season's worth of ballet performances, odds are you've been spending too many nights with the boys. The idea here is that you can get a sense of the type of offense you've committed, and then begin your apology with general references to that type of offense. Let her fill in the specifics, and before you know it you'll understand exactly why she's pissed off.

In the Know

Once you know what it is you're apologizing for, you can begin the apology proper. Apologizing is an art, not a science, so I'll just provide some basic guidelines to follow. It's up to you to sell the performance. One way to do this is to borrow a technique that Method actors use, where you recall a time when you actually were really sorry for something, and try to use that feeling and emotion whenever you need to apologize. Now that you're in character, let's begin.

The good people at SharpMan.com—an excellent source of lifestyle advice for men—have put together a road map to help you through your apology. By the way, if at any point during this process she starts laughing uncontrollably, you may want to forgo the remaining steps and get your sorry ass to the jewelry store, pronto.

Step 1: De-escalate

The decisions you make and the words you use in these first crucial moments will make the difference between détente and escalation into a full-on fight. Watch your body language so you don't give the impression that you're digging in. Don't stick out your chest and cross your arms in front of you. Keep a relaxed posture so you don't make her defensive. Your first words should acknowledge that she may be right (of course, you know she's completely right, but you don't want to give away the farm right off). You may want to summarize the charges against you in your own words, which gives you a chance to level the playing field a bit. She'll be so stunned that you've given some ground that things will settle down into a civilized discussion.

Step 2: Apologize, Sort Of

Once you've opened the channels of communication, you'll want to give a sort of pre-apology, which acknowledges the fact that you've upset her, without actually apologizing for what you've done.

Step 3a: The Mannish Inquisition

If you're still not completely clear what it was about your moronic actions that upset her, this is the time to find out. Tell her that you really want to understand exactly what upset her. It may be that she's been frustrated about something totally unrelated, but your stupidity sent her over the edge. Find that out. No reason to accept more blame than you actually deserve. You may even get her to apologize to you!

Step 3b: The Eventual Honesty

If it's perfectly clear why she's upset, asking her why she's upset will probably just make things worse. In this case, you'll want to skip straight to the self-flagellation portion of our program. Before you tell her exactly why you did what you did, take a moment to admit that you had a momentary lapse of sanity (yeah, it started right after you got back from your honeymoon). That will cushion the blow of your explanation, and you can share all the sordid details. You're going for maximum sympathy here, so put on your most pitiful expression, and would it kill you to conjure up a tear or two? (Pull out a nose hair when she's not looking.) Odds are she'll either understand why you did what you did, figure it was just temporary insanity, or think you're just a pitiful mess. Regardless, you're halfway to make-up sex. Stay focused.

Step 4: Let's Make a Deal

While you're still controlling the negotiation, make a compromise offer that you both can live with. You probably don't need to give in completely, unless you've committed a major offense. So, lay down some ground rules that will give you some breathing room and give her peace of mind as you move forward.

Step 5: Sweeten the Pot

Tell her how important it is that you can have these open and honest conversations with her, and how much you appreciate her understanding. In other words, lay it on thick, brother.

Step 6: For Her, a "Consideration"

In legal jargon, a "consideration" is the transfer of some goods or services that makes the agreement legally binding. In this case, you've got to seal the deal with flowers or a small gift. Make-up sex does not qualify as a consideration because, let's face it, she's getting the short end of the stick on that one (so to speak).

The Postmortem

So, how'd it go? Did she buy it? Did she get the giggles? Regardless of how you got there, you made it through, and that's a victory in its own right. Remember, even the guy who graduates last in his med-school class is still a doctor, and any accepted apology, regardless of how it is accepted, counts as a win.

How to Notice Her New Haircut

This is a fascinating subject for a couple of reasons. First, it illustrates one of the stark differences between women and men. Women gauge the quality of their hair, often several times a day, with a finely calibrated precision instrument that would make a nanotechnologist squint. Their mood, their self-esteem, and the very core of their existence hinges on where, exactly, this particular hair-moment falls on that scale. For men, hair is basically a yes-or-no proposition. And even that question requires that the issue actually breach consciousness before he can answer. Actually, a better title for this subject would be "How to Notice Hair. Period."

Another interesting point about this subject is that it marks an important boundary in the matrimonial encounter. On one side is just how stupid men can be. On the other side is how stupid women *think* men can be. As noted above, men are stupid enough to not notice something as important to their wives as hair. We are not, as women might believe, stupid enough to notice and not say anything. Either way, we're in trouble.

Most men would actually notice a very drastic change in hair color or style (remember when the Philadelphia Phillies all got perms back in the early '80s?), but that happens too infrequently to help the situation much. Unfortunately the mind of man just can't grasp things like highlights, shininess, layers, and roots. So, as usual, we have to figure out a way to trick her into believing we care about her hair.

Going with the theory that even a stopped clock is right twice a day, if you pretend to notice her hair on a preset schedule, you're bound to be right eventually. Of course, there are things you can do to make the whole process a little less random.

First, tell her friends you want to give her a day of beauty, and you're wondering when she's due for her next haircut. They'll give you the full report: date of her last haircut, name of stylist, subject matter of discussion with stylist, price, amount of tip she left, what she bought on her way home, and most important, the date of her next appointment. Once you've got that, you're all set.

Note the date on your calendar, and be sure to tell her how great her hair looks when you see her afterward. Then, set a reminder at about that same interval. Err a bit on the conservative side, since it doesn't matter if you compliment her a few days early, just recover by saying you think her hair looks great as it is, and she should consider letting it grow out a bit. You just want to be sure you don't let a haircut go by without noticing.

As with so many things in this book, the risk in noticing that first haircut is that she's going to expect this kind of treatment every time. Fortunately, it does get easier as you keep doing it, and over time she'll cut you some slack based on your stellar track record.

How to Win Over Her Parents

I read somewhere that Al Gore was an old person's idea of what an ideal young person should be like. Can you imagine what an old person's idea of what an ideal son-in-law would be like? It'd be like Al Gore without the whimsy. Luckily for you, your in-laws gave up being idealists right around the time their daughter announced her engagement.

First and foremost, your in-laws want you to treat their daughter right. You can do that by making gobs and gobs of money or spending every waking moment dedicated to her happiness (or both). If the money just ain't gonna happen, then concentrate on the happiness part.

Keep in mind that a big side effect of being the perfect husband is that it automatically makes you the perfect son-in-law. So be sure to show off all your newly acquired skills whenever you're around the in-laws. Desserts are always big winners, so whip up a little tiramisu (page 178) or, if you're feeling particularly brazen, crème brûlée (page 180). Better still, make the entire meal, set the table yourself (page 154), and then clean up afterward (see "How to Do the Dishes," page 182). Basically, you should take every opportunity to relieve your wife of any domestic responsibility while her parents are around. Sure, they'll know it's not always like this, but they'll appreciate the show, which leads us to the other expectation they have of you.

Beyond treating their daughter right, your in-laws expect

you to treat them right. Hopefully they're drinkers, in which case your job is easy. Make sure whenever you visit them that you bring a bottle of their favorite booze with you, and that you've got their favorite drink chilling when they arrive at your place. If they're not drinkers, just ask your wife about other hobbies and interests they have, and make them your own. Never played mah-jongg? You're in for a treat.

Of course, the best thing you can do is write a book about being the perfect husband and then ask her father to show you how to crack an egg with one hand. If that's not an option, just ask their advice on anything. Sure, you'll get a lecture about how things were done back in their day, but just nod and smile, and keep the martinis flowing, and everything will turn out fine.

How to Explain Football

"**How is football** played?" is right up there with "Do I look fat?" on the list of her idiocy-eliciting inquiries. I'm not suggesting your wife is some treacherous harpy, intent on making you look and feel stupid, but it's possible she may not really be interested in knowing about football at all. She may, in fact, just want to hear you stutter and stumble as you try to explain a game she knows is completely ridiculous (in other words, make you look and feel stupid).

Of course, she may sincerely want to know about the subtle complexities of the game of football. If that's the case, you need to take advantage of this opportunity and explain the game quickly and clearly. Otherwise, you'll miss your chance to finally bring her over to the dark side, and she'll belittle your Sunday rituals even more than she did before.

Either way, you must be prepared with a reasonably coherent explanation of the game. This may sound simple, but if you've never tried it, you'll be amazed at how difficult it is.

Here's a question that belies the difficulty of explaining football: When did you first learn the rules of the game? Can't remember, can you? It's just something you've always known, and that's one of the reasons that it's so hard to explain. Another reason is that, despite the hard-hitting physical image of the game, there are a lot of subtleties and complexities to it.

Try this exercise to illustrate the difficulty of the task at hand. When the game starts, grab the dog (or better yet, the cat), and try to explain the game to him as it's happening. You have before you a creature that knows nothing of the game of football. Every motion, penalty, and play call is a new phenomenon. You'll explain what's happening on the field, and you'll get that blank stare (dog) or contemptuous glare (cat). Either way, you've got more work to do. You'll soon find that explaining football is a royal pain in the ass.

If you want more practice, invite a European friend over for the game, and try explaining it to him. But remember, Europeans feel the same way about football as we do about soccer. So you've still got your work cut out for you. If you can leave Gunter or Olaf or whomever with an appreciation of the game, you may just be ready to try it on the wife.

Do not, under any circumstances, invite your friends over when you're trying to explain the game. This is one time when it needs to be just the two of you. The consequences could be devastating for your relationship with your wife, your friends, or most likely, both.

The first important rule for explaining football to your wife is: Always begin your explanation before kickoff. You've got to lay out the fundamentals before the game begins, otherwise you'll never keep up with the action and she'll get totally frustrated. During the pregame show is a perfect time to begin. If she sits through those inane pregame ramblings, she's only going to realize how stupid this game really is. So, have a late breakfast, turn off the TV, and find a comfy chair in which to explain the game.

When you first begin explaining the sport, don't get too specific. You can leave the details until during the game. For example, there's no way you could explain something as basic as a fair catch ahead of time. Start with such introductory topics as offense vs. defense, kickoffs vs. punts, home jerseys vs. away jerseys, and why linemen have such enormous asses (you know she's going to ask). You may also want to mention the names of the key players (quarterback, running back, head coach). With all of this basic information in hand, she'll have a good general sense of what's going on when the game starts. Then, during the game, you can field all her specific questions.

In order to best prepare yourself for game time, repeat after me: No, honey, that's not a stupid question . . . No, honey, that's not a stupid question . . . No, honey, that's not a stupid question. Good, now you're ready for kickoff.

It can be very frustrating to answer questions in the middle of the game. If you've got TiVo, this is the perfect time to use it. You can pause, rewind, and replay particular plays and explain very clearly exactly what's going on. Otherwise, use instant replay to your advantage. You've got a good sense of when there will be a replay. With the help of John Madden's coloring book scribblings across the screen, you can answer her questions.

This brings us to another issue you'll have to face: the Madden Factor. Your wife can feel only one of two ways about John Madden. She'll either think he's the Will Rogers of play-by-play, or she'll think he's a complete moron. Be prepared to answer each claim. If he's Will Rogers, say something about the populist appeal of football in these troubled times, and Madden's role as an exuberant man-child. If he's a complete moron, just agree and go get her another beer.

Finally, don't give her too much insight into the true extent of your football obsession. Only let her sit in on home games at first, and avoid any mention of rotisserie leagues or Sports Center. That way, she'll think that there's actually some good reason to get excited about these games, other than the fact that they briefly fill that gaping void in your otherwise pathetic, vacuous life.

How to Make More Money

Studies show that married men make upward of 40 percent more money than single guys with comparable experience and education. What the data don't explain is why. Is it because guys who get married are more likely to be creative, go-getter types who thrive under pressure and perform above and beyond the call? Or are they just spending every waking moment in the office because their wives married the hell out of them and they'd rather be anywhere else other than at home? Or is it that they've all been forced to earn more under threat of spousal smackdown and sexual privation (or, possibly even worse, sexual fulfillment)?

Regardless of why it happens, once you're married you apparently have to start doing your part to keep the numbers up. Otherwise, we wouldn't have anything on all those carefree single bastards.

Jack Chapman, a veteran career consultant and author of *Negotiating Your Salary: How to Make $1,000 a Minute*, is a renowned expert at helping people make more money. Whether you're interviewing for a new job or looking to move up within your current company, Chapman has plenty of great advice that really pays off:

1. *Always negotiate:* "While it's true," Chapman says, "that anyone can negotiate salary, it's even more true that everyone *should* negotiate salary." Regardless of your position or pay, you should never say okay to an initial salary offer. Instead, Chap-

man recommends that you "say 'Hmmm' instead, and watch what happens." The fact is, the initial offer will always be at the low end of the spectrum, and negotiating will get you not only a higher salary but also more respect from your employer.

2. *Know what you're worth:* Whenever Chapman is coaching clients, he always tells them straight away that "their negotiation strength comes from knowing what they're worth." There are two measures that determine your value: First, find your objective value by researching salary surveys and other measures for your position. Second, determine your individual value, or your "competitive value," relative to your peers in your company or other close competitors. Finally, recognize that you are always increasing in value to your employer.

3. *Never believe you can't get a raise:* Even if your company has just laid people off or instituted a pay freeze, you can still get a raise. "Most people who survive a reduction in force, or RIF," Chapman says, "don't realize they're worth more to the company after the layoffs." First, there's a reason they weren't laid off, and second, after the RIF there's more work to be done with fewer people. If there's a pay freeze in place, Chapman suggests you try to reclassify or rename your job by taking on more responsibility, thereby bumping yourself up into a higher pay range.

4. *Cash isn't everything:* A raise is not always money. It can come in many forms. Sure, your wife would probably like to see a bigger paycheck, but she might also be happy with more vacation time, a company car, or some extra time off around that client meeting in Hawaii (assuming she's coming with you).

5. *Ride those coattails:* "The best way to become successful yourself," Chapman says, "is to let your boss know that the key to your personal success is doing everything you can to make him or her successful." You can accomplish this during your interview or performance reviews by asking your future or cur-

rent boss this question: "What would you like me to do in my job so that when your boss reviews you, you get a five-star performance review?"

To find out more about Jack Chapman, visit his website, www.salarynegotiations.com, or give him a call at 773-4-SALARY.

How to Deal with PMS and Menopause

> *"An archaeologist is the best husband a woman can have.*
> *The older she gets, the more interested he is in her."*
> —AGATHA CHRISTIE

You'll be relieved to know we're setting the bar really low on this one, guys. Basically, all you have to do is not make matters much, much worse. Don't say or do anything incredibly stupid or insensitive, and make sure you're around and accessible when she needs you, and you can get through this. I promise.

Your first task is to become an informed husband. You'll be amazed at how much better you become at dealing with her apparent possession by satanic demons once you understand what's really going on. Otherwise you'll probably find yourself flipping through the Yellow Pages to *E* for "Exorcist." Luckily, there are some great books out there that clearly explain not only what she's going through but also what you as the husband should do to preserve your marriage and dissuade her from smothering you with a pillow one night.

Probably the best book to get is *Your Guy's Guide to Gynecology*, by Bruce Bekkar and Udo Wahn. This book is a comprehensive guide to the female anatomy and all its myriad repercussions, written for guys who "think that a vulva is a Swedish sports sedan." It deals with PMS and menopause in a chapter aptly entitled "Attack of the Killer Hormones." Read this book, and make sure your wife sees you reading this book. You'll learn everything you need to know about your wife's body. And, once you've seen what a speculum actually looks like, you'll never doubt her tales of gynecological woe ever again. Here are some tips from *Your Guy's Guide to Gynecology* for dealing with PMS:

1. Since stress can exacerbate the effects of PMS, you should do whatever you can to help her relax during this time. If that means helping out more around the house, then do it. Basically, your investment in her relaxation will pay dividends in the form of your own preserved sanity.

2. Her apparent insanity is not something she's doing to you—it's not completely under her control—nor is it something she's thrilled to be going through. She may even feel guilty. So be sympathetic, not defensive. Engage with her, and listen to her (see "How to Listen," page 29).

3. Get out and exercise with her, or make sure she can get some time to go to the gym. Physical activity will go a long way toward making her feel better.

4. Help her avoid sweets, salty foods, caffeine, and alcohol, and encourage her to eat frequent small meals rather than a few big ones. All this will help minimize the symptoms of PMS.

A great book that deals with just menopause is Dick Roth's *"No, It's Not Hot in Here": A Husband's Guide to Understanding Menopause*. Roth goes into great detail about the physiology and psychology of menopause, the science and controversies surrounding it, and how it can affect your relationship. Roth's ultimate goal is to help husbands understand what's going on and what they should and shouldn't do to help their wives through this process. "Remember," he says, "there's nothing wrong with her. She's just going through the menopause, so there's nothing to fix. You are not a mechanic; you're her husband." Here are some tips from *"No, It's Not Hot in Here"* for dealing with menopause:

1. Definitely educate yourself about menopause. It's an amazing process, and can be scary as hell. You and your wife

need to go through this together, with a complete understanding of what's happening.

2. Remember, there's nothing to fix here, and you probably don't have any answers anyway. Just be supportive, ask a lot of questions, and listen to her.

3. Menopause can have significant sexual side effects. Many women experience a decreased sex drive (although some experience an increase). Don't take it personally. If you've followed steps 1 and 2 above, it's probably the menopause, not something you've done that's turned her off. Be patient. When she does want to have sex, recognize that her diminished estrogen levels can cause slower lubrication. Once again, be patient, and plan on using a water-based lubricant like K-Y or Astroglide. Luckily for you, the conventional wisdom is that sex will become easier the more you do it.

4. Be involved. Participate in her medical consultations and remind her to take her medications on schedule. Improve your diet and exercise regimens together.

Remember, guys, it's quite possible that you'll be going through some serious life transitions at the same time (see "How to Have a Reasonable Midlife Crisis," page 23). Don't let your own issues cause you to get defensive or distant with her. Use this time to grow together, not apart. So, if there's a new little red sports car in the garage, you may want to let her drive it every once in a while, too (but before you do, be sure to read "How to Appear Calm When She's Driving," page 192).

SEX AND ROMANCE

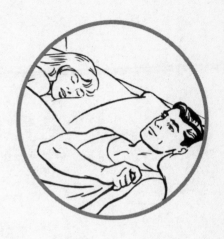

How to Find the Perfect Gift

The first law of gift-giving is that any gift given spontaneously, for no particular reason is, by definition, perfect. The second law, unfortunately, is that no amount of spontaneous gift-giving will compensate for even a single crappy gift on her birthday or your anniversary. So you should take any opportunity to thrill her with little gifts throughout the year. Just don't expect any leniency when she unwraps that toaster oven on her birthday. The simple fact is that even though you should always buy her gifts throughout the year, you've got to go above and beyond for the big events.

You'll need to find at least two or three great gifts every year (birthday, anniversary, and Christmas/Hanukkah). There are two main categories of gifts from which you can choose: things and experiences. Things are easier to acquire, but are less memorable. Experiences take more leg work, but have a greater "wow" factor.

If your wife is laying down some serious hints that there's something she really wants, you damn well better deliver. Of course, she's setting you up for failure, since the best you're likely to do is just meet her expectations. So, you've got to go above and beyond. If she's expecting a piece of jewelry (see "How to Buy Jewelry," page 59), have the maître d' at your restaurant deliver it with dessert (you *have* already made reservations at someplace special, haven't you?). If she wants new skis, pick her up from work on Friday with them already on the roof rack, wrapped up with a bow, and whisk her off to the slopes for the weekend. If she loves flowers, have a bouquet delivered every month for a year.

Now, if your wife hasn't given you any clues, don't panic. Seize this opportunity to deliver something truly memorable: an experience she'll remember forever. The two main categories of experiences are evenings out and trips. Don't have any ideas? Don't worry. Take a minute to think about a memorable meal you had in the past, a trip you took way back when, her favorite movie, TV show, book, whatever. Now you've got plenty of ideas.

Remember that special meal you two had when you first started dating? You could take her back to the same place, or you could bring the place to you. Try hiring a personal chef to re-create that memorable meal at home. Contact the American Personal Chef Association (www.personalchef.com) or the U.S. Personal Chef Association (www.hireachef.com) for more information.

How about trips? Remember your first getaway together? Or has she always talked about a trip she took in college, and how she'd love to go back there with you? Most airlines sell package deals to lots of major cities, including airfare, hotel, and even meals.

She'd probably love a weekend getaway at a bed-and-breakfast somewhere. Check BBonline.com, find one nearby, and book it for that special weekend. Ask the folks at the inn if there are any nice restaurants nearby that they'd recommend. They may also have some pull to get you a reservation or a great table. Also, be sure to tell them you're celebrating a special occasion. They may bump you up to a better room.

Another strategy is to pay attention to her favorite movies, TV shows, and books. It will take some work, but you could plan something based on a particular favorite. She loved *About a Boy*? There are lots of weekend deals to London.

She can't turn off the *Eukanuba Tournament of Champions*? Take her to a dog show in New York. Is she addicted to the Food Network? Enroll in cooking classes (together, of course). If your wife loves tennis, get tickets to a local USTA tournament (don't get tickets to the Anna Kournikova match, that's just too obvious).

Or try planning a getaway close to home. Many of the big hotels do most of their business during the week with corporate clients. So they occasionally offer incentives to get people in for the weekend. Get online and check their websites. Book a weekend, which will probably include the room, dinner, breakfast, and some other perk like tickets to a show. One phone call, and you've got a great gift she'll love.

Finally, as a last resort, try eBay. It's an amazing resource for stuff you never knew existed. Just search on anything she might be interested in, and you're almost guaranteed to find any number of items to bid on. If you know her favorite author, see if you can find an autographed first edition. Or, better still, try to find some lost heirloom from her childhood, like a rare stuffed animal or toy she loved.

Forget Her Not (or You're Dead Meat)

Now that you know how to find her a great gift, you've got to remember to buy it for her well in advance of the big day. One useful strategy is to backtrack from her birthday, your anniversary, or Christmas/Hanukkah, and find another holiday about a month or so prior. Then, use that holiday as your reminder to get in gear and find her a gift for the upcoming big one. For example, my anniversary is October 9, so I use Labor Day as a reminder to start thinking about anniversary plans. You can also automate the whole process if you do a lot of shopping online. Many of the big e-tailers, like Amazon.com, let you set up reminders of important upcoming dates.

The key here is to really be creative, and customize everything to her. Remember that for most women, the personal touch is worth a lot, so expend a little energy and save yourself some cash.

How to Buy Jewelry

Difficulty

T T T

Reward

♥ ♥ ♥ ♥

According to a recent study conducted by Blue Nile, an online diamond and fine jewelry retailer, 75 percent of men said they don't feel knowledgeable about buying jewelry. And yet, men still do most of the jewelry purchasing. Now, what does that tell you? Here's an entire gender that knows every trivial spec about their cars, their stereos, even their fishing rods, and yet they drop down hundreds if not thousands of dollars for jewelry without any research whatsoever. If that doesn't prove once and for all that women have won the battle of the sexes, I don't know what will. There's really no way to remedy the situation and remain married, so at least we can educate ourselves a bit and see if we can avoid getting ripped off in the process.

First, let's familiarize ourselves with the different materials we're likely to encounter:

Gold

The purity of gold is expressed in units called "karats," with each karat representing $\frac{1}{24}$ of the total. So, 24 karat gold (24k) is 100 percent gold. But because gold is very soft, other metals are added to make an alloy hard enough for use as jewelry, usually resulting in 14k or 18k gold. Keep in mind that solid gold does not mean 24k gold, but a gold object of any karat that is solid metal, and not hollow. When inspecting a piece of gold jewelry, look for the karat mark, as well as the name or trademark of the producer.

Platinum

More expensive than gold, platinum is also mixed with other metals. The purity of platinum is marked in parts of platinum per thousand. If an alloy is more than 950 parts platinum, it may be labeled as just platinum (Plat. or Pt.). Otherwise it will list the number of parts per thousand of platinum. If the platinum content is significantly low, the rating may also list the other composite metals.

Silver

Jewelry made of "sterling silver" is 92.5 percent silver, with other metals (usually copper) added for durability. Look for the quality marks "sterling," "ster," "sterling silver," or "925," all of which must be accompanied by the producer's trademark.

Diamonds

The value of a diamond is determined by its carat (weight), cut, color, and clarity.

Carat: One carat (not to be confused with karats of gold) equals $\frac{1}{5}$ gram.

Cut: The cut of the diamond is not really about the shape of the stone, but about how well it reflects light. The more light that is reflected, the more brilliant the stone appears (and the more expensive it is). Without getting too complicated, just know that "ideal" cuts are the best and most expensive.

Color: Paradoxically, the ideal color for a diamond is no color at all. Diamonds are graded on a color scale, which starts at the most expensive and colorless, indicated by the letter D.

As you move down the alphabet, diamonds get cheaper and more yellow ("fancy colored" diamonds, which may actually have lots of bright color, are very rare and very expensive).

Clarity: A diamond's clarity refers to the amount of internal blemishes, or "inclusions." While a lower clarity grade will affect the price of a diamond, it's very difficult to tell the difference with the naked eye.

Pearls

There are four different types of pearls you may encounter:

Natural pearls are those created by oysters on their own. Natural pearls are extremely rare and very expensive.

Cultured pearls are produced by oysters, but they're made with a little outside assistance. Cultivators insert a small bead into the oyster, which is then coated with "nacre," the substance the oyster produces that forms the pearl and provides its luster.

Freshwater pearls, while often not as perfectly formed as saltwater pearls, do tend to have a thicker coating of lustrous nacre. In addition, they're more reasonably priced than their saltwater cousins.

Imitation pearls are made of plastic or glass, fabricated to look like pearls.

Of course, just knowing a little bit about the components of jewelry doesn't really help all that much with the actual buying process. The most important thing to consider is personal preference. And since you're buying for your wife, it's her preference that really counts. Here are some tips to help you find the perfect jewelry for her:

1. What types of jewelry does she wear, or not wear? If you notice that she only wears gold, then she may not appreciate a silver ring. If she has lots of necklaces and earrings, that's a good sign that she enjoys them. Remember, jewelry is an

irrational pursuit, so as long as you don't buy the exact same thing, the more the better.

2. Look to match with jewelry she already has. Women are always looking to match earrings with a necklace, and vice versa.

3. Try to match an outfit. Buy her pearls to go with that black dress she just bought. Not only do you get points for the jewelry, but you earn extra credit for noticing her clothes.

4. Don't go it alone. Ask family and friends for their suggestions. Spend plenty of time with your jeweler, asking questions and telling him or her about your wife. A little expert advice can go a long way in finding the perfect piece.

5. Make it significant. Buy something to remind her of that trip you took together, or have a family heirloom reset for her to wear. This one can be tricky, so make sure you consult friends and family before purchasing.

Now, when the time comes to buy, the fun really begins. If your wife will appreciate that little blue box from Tiffany's as much as the jewelry inside, then by all means raise your credit limit and head on over. But I would suggest that you shop around in those fancy department stores, and then make the final purchase in the diamond district downtown (most big downtowns have one), in some old brick building where the elevator has a gate you have to slide over manually before the door closes. You know, the kind of a place where you'd expect to see Christian Szell, the "White Angel" from *Marathon Man*, walk by with a briefcase manacled to his wrist. Just keep in mind that when you walk through that door, you have to commit yourself to haggling like you're in a Turkish bazaar, since the salesmen are master closers and it's tough to get out of there without buying something. Here are some suggestions to help you get a great deal:

1. Do your homework, so you know exactly what you're looking for. If they don't have it, move on to the next place.

2. After they show you what they've got, even if you see exactly what you're looking for, always ask, "So, when are you getting more in?"

3. They'll say something like, "The retail on this one is $8,500, but I can let it go for $650." I'm never sure what retailer could ever charge that top number—maybe that's the price in Turkish liras or drachmas or something.

4. As far as you're concerned, there is no bottom to this negotiation. I don't care how offended he pretends to be, you should negotiate as if he'll eventually just give it to you for free.

5. Eventually you'll get to a number that feels like rock bottom. Offer him $20 less. Keep in mind a lot of these places only take cash (surprise, surprise).

6. Most important of all, make sure you know their refund and return policy before any money changes hands. Make sure your receipt has the exact details of the item you bought, along with any certification that may go along with it. Wives are notorious returners and exchangers. She may tell you she's just taking the ring or necklace back for a fitting, and come back with something completely different and assume you'll never notice. If she's happy, then you're happy, so just play dumb.

To use the musical terminology, most jewelry has a strong attack but a limited sustain. You make a great impression when the gift is delivered, but unless it's something she'll wear every day, the effect soon fades. The best way to lengthen the sustain is to associate the jewelry with another memorable event. See "How to Find the Perfect Gift" (page 55) for tips to help you create a memorable getaway in which to present her with the jewelry, and thus make the jewelry more memorable, too.

How to Wrap a Gift

Gift wrapping demands a deft touch, a sense of flair and panache, and an appreciation of those frilly and ephemeral accents that add spice to life. In other words, it's something guys suck at, and have no interest in not sucking at. It's just something you've got to do. You don't ever want to lessen the impact of your gift just because it's poorly wrapped in the Sunday funnies. Luckily, you've got a lot of options short of actually wrapping the gift yourself.

First, shop online at places that offer a gift wrapping service. There's no easier way to gift wrap a present than to click on "Gift wrap it!" Amazon.com does a nice job gift wrapping, as do specialty gift stores like RedEnvelope.com.

If you're out shopping at a store, always ask if they'll gift wrap your purchase. Most reputable retailers offer this service either for free or for a nominal charge. Regardless of the price, it's worth it.

If the task of wrapping rests in your meaty, maladroit mitts, you can still get away without actually wrapping. If the gift is relatively small, you can stop into one of those card shops and purchase a nice gift bag and some white tissue paper. Just put a few layers of tissue in the bag, place the gift inside, and then cover with more tissue paper, poofed up in nice wispy peaks.

If your gift is larger or in a sizable box, it must be wrapped. If you're faced with no other options than doing it yourself, rest assured that it's not that difficult. As with making a bed, you should visualize this as a construction project, to move it into a manlier realm.

Here's how it's done:

1. First, make sure you've got a roll of nice, stylish wrapping paper. If all you've got in the house is last year's Christmas paper with snowmen and reindeer, go out to the store and get something nice.

2. Cut about four or five pieces of tape, each about three inches long, and carefully stick one end of each piece on a handy surface near your work area (and not on the end table your wife just refinished).

3. Roll out enough paper to cover the top of your box, then place the box upside down on the paper. Keep unrolling as you bring the paper up and over the box, then down the other side. Roll out a few more inches and cut the paper at that point. Straighten out the paper and place the box in the center.

4. Fold the long sides up onto the box, so they overlap by a few inches. Pull them taut and secure with a piece of clear tape.

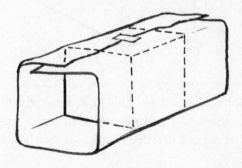

5. Turn the box so one of the open sides is facing you. Fold the top flap down along the edge of the box, then fold each of the two side flaps in. Make a tight crease on either side of the bottom flap, pressing down on your work surface. Then, fold the bottom flap up and tape it to the side of the box. Repeat on the other side, and you're all done.

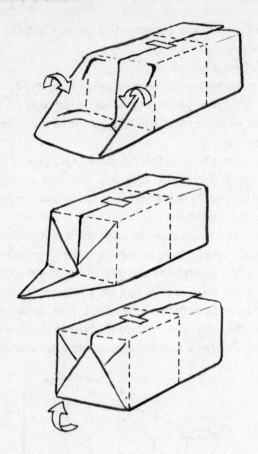

And don't forget a card. This time, forget the joke card or the poetic drivel. Get a blank card with a nice image on the front and write her a heartfelt note inside. See how easy it is to be "da man"?

How to Make a Bouquet

If we were to create a superhero costume for Perfect Husband Man, it would have to include some sort of built-in mechanism that would allow him to whip out a fresh bouquet of flowers at a moment's notice. When Perfect Husband Man feels like getting his wife a spontaneous gift just because he loves her—WHAM—there'd be a bouquet at the ready. When Perfect Husband Man forgets to record the *Sex and the City* marathon because he's watching SlamBall—SOCKO—flowers make the apology stick. You see, guys, flowers are the perfect husband's best friend. They're versatile, effective, and practically immune to womanly skepticism. You can use flowers to apologize for the same offense over and over again, and somehow she'll keep falling for it. It's as if the sight and smell of flowers interferes with her built-in bullshit detector, and you're home free every time.

Since there is no Perfect Husband Man costume—and even if there were, you wouldn't want to know where the vase is stored—here are some tips to help you buy, arrange, and care for flowers (with thanks to the good people at the California Cut Flower Commission for many of these suggestions):

1. Roses always work. It doesn't matter what color they are or how they're arranged. You can't go wrong. Look for blooms that are only about halfway opened (closed flowers may never open, and fully opened flowers may not last very long).

2. When you go to the florist to buy a flower arrangement, tell them why you're buying the flowers and what sentiment you want to express. Talk about her favorite flowers and colors and where you think the arrangement will be displayed in your house. Finally, make sure you let them know your budget and ask about any additional costs that may be included.

3. If you're just buying cut flowers to bring home, make sure you take care of them so they'll last as long as possible. First, be sure to get some flower food from the florist (they should include a little packet with your flowers). Find a vase that's large enough to hold the flowers, and about half their height. Fill the vase halfway with water and stir in the flower food until it dissolves. Remove any leaves that don't come above the water level in the vase. Then hold the stems under water and cut

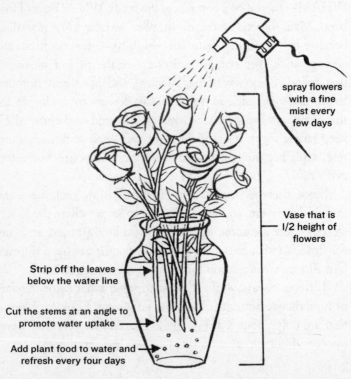

spray flowers with a fine mist every few days

Vase that is 1/2 height of flowers

Strip off the leaves below the water line

Cut the stems at an angle to promote water uptake

Add plant food to water and refresh every four days

them on an angle with sharp scissors. You should change the water every four days or so (adding fresh food and reclipping the bottoms of the stems), and you should spray flowers with a fine mist of water every couple of days to keep them fresh.

4. When buying flowers for the dinner table, you don't want them too tall, because you want to be able to see across the table.

5. If you're making breakfast in bed, you absolutely must have flowers to set the mood. Since space is at a premium, you'll want to use a small, narrow vase (called a "bud vase") or a champagne flute. Place one or two dramatic flowers in the vase and bring it to the bedroom when you deliver the coffee. Flowers add just the right touch of elegance to breakfast in bed, and the scent makes the meal even more enjoyable.

6. Don't place your flowers in direct sunlight, too close to a heat source, or in a drafty spot. If you've got pets or small children, be sure to place the flowers out of their reach. And, of course, don't place them on the television or any electrical appliance.

7. Flowers can make the perfect gift, even for very special occasions. You just have to think big. Check your wedding photos or call the florist that did your wedding, and have them make up an arrangement of the same flowers your wife had in her bouquet. Or give flowers all year round with a bouquet-of-the-month gift.

For more information on flowers and flower arranging, visit the California Cut Flower Commission's website at www.ccfc.org.

How to Give a Foot Massage

Difficulty
1

Reward
♥ ♥ ♥ ♥

If you don't already give your wife regular, spontaneous foot rubs, you're missing a great opportunity. From her perspective, a good foot massage (and it's almost impossible to give a bad one) not only feels great, but it's also a tacit acknowledgment of the rigors of modern womanhood. If she's a stay-at-home mom, there's no better way to express your appreciation for all the hard work that job entails. If she has a career, a foot rub can be a political statement, expressing your solidarity and outrage that society still forces women to wear nonsensible shoes. *Semper commodum!* Hoo-ah!

After a foot rub, she'll feel relaxed and appreciated, and you'll get a blank check for any number of otherwise forbidden activities. If you're still not convinced, then just think of a foot rub as a great hand-strengthening exercise. A simple, ten-minute workout can improve your golf game, your jump shot, and also allow you to stay out late with the boys Saturday night.

There are some tricks to giving a great foot rub, but remember that any foot rub counts, so don't worry too much about it.

1. Ask your wife what she would like and wouldn't like. The foot can be a touchy subject, and you don't want to start off by making her uncomfortable. She may prefer to have socks on or soak her feet first. Or the toes may be way too ticklish to touch. Figure that all out ahead of time.

2. The right pressure is key to a good foot rub. Go too light and it may be too ticklish, too hard and it can really hurt. Sit on

opposite sides of the couch facing each other, hold her foot in both hands, and give a firm overall massage of the entire foot. Then, with your thumbs underneath and fingers wrapped around on top, apply a rolling pressure with your thumbs to the entire sole of her foot. Be careful not to pull or stretch the skin on top of her foot, which can be very painful. Just work on kneading the fleshy part of the foot, working from front to the back. You may want to pay particular attention to the heel.

Be careful not to pinch or stretch here

Steady, firm pressure here

3. Using a massage cream can make your job easy. Find a cream with mint and/or eucalyptus, which can do amazing things to soothe aching feet. Just gently rub some of that on and your work is pretty much complete.

4. You may also want to move her feet and toes through their full range of motion to loosen up the joints. Do this carefully, and make sure you don't force any joint beyond its natural range of motion. As you extend her foot forward, toward you, work your thumbs gently down between the tendons on top of the foot.

5. If she feels comfortable with it, massage the toes individually, and in between the toes.

6. As with all endeavors involving physical contact, pay

attention to her reactions. If she turns to Jell-O, you've found a good spot. If she pulls away quickly, you've probably found a sensitive spot that can either be ticklish or particularly sore. Sore spots may need extra attention, but you've got to be gentle. Ticklish spots may be handled with firm, steady pressure, or should be avoided altogether.

Once again, it proves to be so easy to please her, and to get something out of it for yourself. Just remember, when you're out with the boys and they want to know what you did to get a free pass from the wife, you may want to embellish a bit.

How to Hide Your Porn

Believe it or not, there are women out there who appreciate and enjoy pornography. If you're not married to either of them, you'd best keep your stash well hidden. The most effective strategies for the twenty-first-century pornophile can be summed up in two words: Go digital.

Move to DVDs

The jump from videos to DVDs is not just a revolution in sound and picture quality (as well as in scanning convenience), but also presents the greatest advance in porn concealment since the invention of the mattress. Here's how it works:

1. Go to your local Staples or OfficeMax and buy a bunch of double-disk jewel cases for CDs.

2. Grab a few of your CDs off the shelf, open up the cases, and pop out the disk holders.

3. Replace them with the new double-disk holder, and conceal the DVD in the hidden space in the back for the second CD.

4. Close the insert, replace the original CD, and return the case to its spot.

Of course, as with videos, the central challenge is not necessarily keeping the disks hidden, but remembering to remove them from the player and put them back afterward. This is a tough one to get around, especially considering that the male

brain can't even control basic motor skills while orchestrating an orgasm, let alone remember to put the DVD back. Your best bet here is to pin a note to your sleeve that reads "Put your porn away, jackass!"

Keep in mind that this is a very versatile maneuver, and can be used for things other than porn. For example, if you're a closet Britney Spears or Patrick Swayze fan, you can always use this technique to hide bubblegum pop and chick flicks behind your Grand Funk Railroad and Mötley Crüe CDs, or any other disks you know she'll never open.

Get Online

Now, online porn seems like the panacea men have been waiting for. The problem with online porn is that much of your activity online is easy to deduce. One way to cover your tracks is to delete the "history" on your browser. Your history is found in the drop-down box at the top of the browser window, and shows all the URLs you've visited recently. Of course, deleting all your history is just as conspicuous as leaving www.pornmakesmylifebearable.com out there for all to see. So, after you delete your history, be sure to do a little nonporn surfing so it's not too obvious that you're hiding something. If you use Internet Explorer, here's how to delete your history:

At the very top of your browser, click "Tools" and select "Internet Options."

Click the "Clear History" button and then click "Yes" to confirm the command.

If you use a different browser, just search the "Help" index to find out how to delete your lurid browsing history.

Before You Trash Your Old Stash

Now don't go throwing away all your old magazines and videos just yet. They've still got some life left in them. Gather everything together, pack it up in a box, and be sure the top is securely taped closed. Label it somewhat conspicuously (something only slightly more covert than "My Secret Porn Stash" will do) and keep it "hidden" in a place where your wife is sure to find it. When she does find it, two things can happen (both of which work in your favor).

Outcome A: She'll be shocked and appalled. In this case you sheepishly state, "I haven't looked at that stuff since we got married," making sure she notices the packing tape, and throw it all away. You get points for self-improvement, and she feels personally responsible for it.

Outcome B: She'll give you a sly grin and start flipping through your stash. In this case, you've hit the jackpot and you won't be needing my help anymore!

How to Pull an "Encore Performance"

Believe it or not, there are several companies out there offering products that purport to assist in the manly arts of love. Who knew? Why, even this morning, in my very own e-mail inbox, I received several offerings from such reputable outfits—which I assume are closely regulated by the FDA and, in some cases, the American Sport Horse Association—claiming they would distend my genitals to equine proportions, make my woman scream with glee upon unleashing my "massive man meat," and/or help me crush any number of beverage receptacles with my "rock hard ramburglar." And it's not even my birthday! I've even received messages, now get this, claiming that men can satisfy their women, not just the obligatory once a week, but twice in the same night! I know it sounds ridiculous, but it's true!

In fact, there are several possible strategies to employ to achieve this miraculous task. Some have been used for thousands of years. From what I can gather, they were originally employed by some sect of particularly horny shamans in Tibet or somewhere.

Other, more recently discovered methods, such as Kegel exercises, utilize muscle conditioning to prolong stamina. Seems like a manly enough pursuit. It's worth noting, though, that these exercises (of the pubococcygeus, or PC muscle) were originally used to help with postpartum incontinence in women. Maybe if you thought about that instead of baseball, you wouldn't have this problem in the first place. But that's really a different issue. What we're looking for is the encore performance, not just a single marathon session.

Another technique utilizes the distinction between orgasm and ejaculation (yes, it's true, they are different things). With proper instruction and training, you can achieve multiple orgasms through the course of the night, and "release the hounds" only when you're good and ready. Once again, that's not technically a repeat performance, and it seems to me with this method you run the risk of a backfire blowing out your spleen.

So we're left with a couple of other options. The first method is designed to shorten the time in between erections from your normal interval, say 168 hours or so, down to about fifteen minutes. First of all, you've got to get yourself in decent physical condition (see "How to Get Six-Pack Abs," page 15) and avoid drinking or eating a heavy meal that evening. Anybody still with me?

Well, for the few of you remaining, here's the technique: You want to create a connection in your mind, using a form of self-hypnosis, between how you feel just after sex and how you'll feel when you're ready to go again. So, picture in your head an image of yourself, spent and exhausted after sex, and concentrate on a particular physical sensation you feel at that moment. Then, transform that image into one of you wildly engaged in your favorite sex act, with whomever or whatever you find most arousing. The idea is to keep transforming that image in your mind, and it should help you rise to the occasion yet again.

Exercise, sobriety, and self-hypnosis not quite right for you? Then how about masturbation, heavy drinking, and faking it? Bet I've got your attention now.

Women have been faking orgasms for generations. It's time we returned the favor. Of course, the faked male orgasm requires both stamina and subterfuge. If you're normally on a hair trigger, this may not be the technique for you. First, prepare yourself so you can last as long as possible later that night. Sometime during the day, get one round out of the chamber (if you catch my drift). Later that night, be sure to have at least a few drinks. If you've got any other techniques to help slow you down, employ them as well (keep in mind that the use of a condom facilitates this trick).

When the moment is right, be sure the lights are off, and get started. Then, before you're ready to finish, launch into your best orgasm routine: the tensed muscles, the scrunched-up face, the desperate gasps for air, and the final climax. Say something like, "Baby, you were so hot tonight I couldn't hold back." Odds are she'll be so flattered she won't catch on that something's up.

Then, just when she settles in for sleep, you move in for *el numero dos.* The risk in all this is that she'll think you've found your inner stud, and she might expect this kind of treatment all the time. If that's the case, then you have my deepest sympathies. I suggest you forget about baseball, postpartum incontinence, booze, and self-gratification, and just try to get everything over with as quickly as possible. Then heed the words of Dr. Sydney Friedman, the esteemed peripatetic shrink from *M*A*S*H:* "Ladies and gentlemen, take my advice, pull down your pants and slide on the ice."

How to Stay Awake After Sex

Add this to the "Top 100 Reasons Why It's Amazing Men and Women Ever Got Together in the First Place" list: Right after orgasm, both men and women get a big infusion of the hormone oxytocin. Oxytocin gives women a need for physical contact (oxytocin is nicknamed "the cuddle hormone"). So, she's all fired up and ready for some serious snuggling. At the same time, the oxytocin in men is blocked by high levels of testosterone. This increases the effect of another hormone, serotonin, which makes men sleepy. Ain't that a bitch?

Between this little bombshell and the whole multiple orgasm thing, it's getting harder and harder to believe that God is a guy. Of course, only a guy could think up such devious ways to screw over his buddies. Either way, husbands the world over have their work cut out for them every time she demands that postcoital cuddle.

According to Vanessa Burton, women's sexuality correspondent at the online men's portal AskMen.com, there are lots of things you can do to avoid the dreaded "cold roll" that wives have been perfecting for generations. Something as simple as a little caffeine can make all the difference. Have a coffee with dinner, or shotgun a Coke on the way to bed, and you should be able to stay awake for some quality snuggle time. Along those lines, try to avoid big, heavy meals before sex, and keep the alcohol to a minimum.

David Strovny, the sex education correspondent at AskMen.com, suggests that you check your breathing. You're probably holding your breath during orgasm, which will leave you even more worn out afterward. Try to keep your breathing relaxed and deep until the deed is done, and you'll find you have more energy later. Also, try sitting up in bed. Your wife can still get in a decent snuggle position, and you're much less likely to doze off.

Another interesting technique that Burton suggests is starting up an engaging conversation with your wife afterward. And what could be more engaging than to hear her talk about how great you just were? This one's a little risky, but with the proper leading questions, you should be able to elicit a glowing review.

Most important, Burton stresses, if you simply cannot keep your eyes open, be sure to leave her feeling good. Tell her how amazing she was, and that she completely wore you out, and you just can't stay awake.

Of course, if all else fails, rather than trying to stay awake yourself, why not get her to fall asleep? The best way to do this is to get her liquored up before you hop in the sack. That way she'll be so exhausted after you're done, you'll both have no problem dozing off.

How to Make Breakfast in Bed

Making breakfast in bed for your wife is one of the most romantic and charming things you can do for her. But it is a labor fraught with peril, my friend. Fraught, I say. With peril! There is no greater proof that women are treacherous, manipulative beasts bent on the subjugation of man than this idea we've somehow gotten into our heads that they would actually like to eat breakfast in bed. Sure, if it's executed to perfection, they'll enjoy it just fine. But screw it up—and hear me now, there are many, *many* ways in which you can screw it up—and you'll receive that same baneful glare as when you perform less than spectacularly at certain other oral endeavors.

First off, you've got to ease her into breakfast in bed. If you barge in on a sleeping wife, you're asking for trouble. I know if I wake up my wife before she's ready, even with delicious pork products in tow, I'd be fortunate to get away with only minor facial lacerations. Actually, she's considered a viable threat by the local authorities until well into her second cup of coffee. So give your wife time to get washed up, and if she's like some sort of cranky newborn gerbil before her first coffee, make damn sure she gets her fix right off. Also, if she loves the comics or the crossword puzzle, bring those in with the coffee and let her ease into the morning while you get the rest of breakfast ready.

Coffee

Fiddling with a cup of coffee in bed is risky business, and the slightest spill will ruin everything. Learn how she likes her coffee ahead of time, and add the cream and sugar before taking it upstairs. If she's a tea drinker, find out what kind she wants, then prepare it ahead of time as well (but make sure, like coffee, it's served hot). She won't want spent tea bags cluttering up her breakfast tray. It's okay to use a travel mug to avoid spills—or better yet, go out and get one of those wide-bottom mugs made especially for this occasion.

The Breakfast Proper

Now let's get a handle on the whole food thing. First, to dispel a commonly held misconception: Cold cereal is not an appropriate main course for breakfast in bed. For one thing, cereal doesn't smell nearly enough. I don't care if your wife is a fourth-level vegan, no memorable breakfast would be complete without the delicate bouquet of sizzling pork fat. So before you do anything else, heat up a big old skillet and throw in some bacon. Then you can get to work on the rest of the meal. Relax, we'll keep it simple.

BISCUITS
Yes, biscuits. Trust me, they're really easy.
Preheat the oven to 450°.
Combine 2 cups flour, I tablespoon baking powder, and I teaspoon salt in a mixing bowl.
Combine ¾ cup milk and ⅓ cup oil, and then dump it all into the bowl.
Stir it up with a fork just until it all comes together.
Drop six blobs of dough onto an ungreased baking sheet.
Bake for about 12 minutes or until golden brown.

EGGS

We'll just go with scrambled, since there's nothing easier.

Whisk together 3 eggs, a teaspoon of salt, and a tablespoon or two of milk.

Set a skillet over low heat and melt I tablespoon of butter.

When the butter starts to foam, pour in the egg mixture and turn up the heat a bit.

Stir the eggs around in the skillet until they're cooked through but not dry.

Remove the eggs from the heat, and stir in a splash of milk to keep them creamy.

FRUIT SALAD

This one takes the least effort, and will have the greatest impact. Just slice up a bunch of chilled fruit and throw it all together in a nice bowl. To keep things easy, use fruits that require the least prep work: strawberries, grapes, bananas, apples, peaches, and pears.

ORANGE JUICE

You've got to have fresh-squeezed orange juice, but there's nothing that says you have to squeeze it yourself. You'll save a lot of money making your own, but it's a royal pain in the ass. Keep in mind, if you want to make Mimosas (orange juice and champagne), just stick to the cheap stuff.

Presentation

This is a key component of breakfast in bed, and something guys tend to overlook. In this case, not only do you want everything to look nice, but you've got to figure out how she's going to eat everything while sitting in bed. You need to make sure you've either got one of those trays with the fold-out legs made for this purpose, or just use a side table and keep all the food right next to the bed. You'll also need to find out where she keeps the cloth napkins (see "How to Set the Table," page 154), and don't forget that a small vase of flowers is crucial to pulling this whole thing off (see "How to Make a Bouquet," page 67).

This would be a good time to consider one last time if you actually want to go through with this. If you're beginning to realize your wife will absolutely hate the thought of biscuit crumbs and fruit salad soiling her precious bed linens, you may just want to move the whole thing to the dining room.

Finally, and most important of all, you've got to do all the cleaning. Leaving a sinkful of dirty dishes will instantly and completely negate the positive impact of everything you've just done. So use the techniques from "How to Do the Dishes" (page 182), leave the dishwasher open the whole time, and clean as you go. Make sure the cups, plates, and utensils you take to the bedroom are the only dishes remaining to be cleaned after breakfast. Then, when she's all finished, just clear everything from the bedroom, put it all in the dishwasher, and you're done.

The whole thing was a ton of work, but if you followed these guidelines and did everything right, you should now be the deserving recipient of a few oral endeavors from her: a sincere "thank you" and a big, wet smooch.

AROUND THE HOUSE

How to Use the TV Remote Correctly

The key to breaking the gender deadlock surrounding the remote control centers on the very thing that prompted physicist Robert Adler to create the first remote for Zenith in the 1950s: commercials. The first remote control was intended to allow viewers to mute the television during commercials and/ or change channels to avoid them altogether. Focusing on the commercial breaks in our television viewing, and remembering the original intention of this revolutionary device, we can address one of the longest-standing disputes between husband and wife.

There are lots of theories about why men hog the remote and channel surf more than women. Maybe Jerry Seinfeld was right. Maybe men's primal instinct is to hunt, while women's is to nest, and that's why we have radically different approaches to the remote. Maybe it's because men have a shorter attention span and a greater need for constant stimulation. Maybe it's because the remote provides one of the few remaining outlets for men's desperate need for control. Or maybe it's as Michael Gurian posits, that biological differences between the male and female brain cause men to seek out different types of stimuli in different ways. He makes a good case, and backs it up with all kinds of, like, evidence and stuff, but I prefer to believe the real reason is that men's mental abilities are so sophisticated, so far advanced beyond those of women, that we're just taking in stimuli at a comfortable pace and she just can't keep up. Yeah, I like that last one, although I wouldn't suggest you share that particular theory with the wife. She may not understand it, what with her limited mental faculties and all.

So we're faced with a dilemma. Should you deny your true talent, and face almost certain boredom, just so your wife won't feel left behind? Of course you *should*, but you obviously haven't volunteered to do so to this point. I know it's hard, but with the simple four-step program we've developed here at Perfect Husband Laboratories, you can learn how to break your habit and find other outlets for your scary talents.

1. *The point is mute:* If you can't get the surfing monkey off your back right away, at least use the remote for its original purpose before you start flipping. Mute the television, which significantly diminishes the sensory impact of the surfing. That way, you get a little fix, and your wife gets an aural respite for a few minutes.

2. *Selective surfing:* If you simply must flip through channels, try to select just your three or four favorites, and jump to them by keying the channel number into the remote (or find a remote that lets you preset several channels into memory). You'll get to see most of what you're interested in, without dragging your wife through millisecond glimpses of every channel in between.

3. *Lap trance:* You know how smokers will substitute gum or toothpicks or some other oral implement for cigarettes to help them quit? Well, the same goes for your mad clicking fingers. Remember that classic Mattel Handheld Football game? Well, you can still find them, either new at places like Circuit City, or used on eBay. When the commercials come on, use the game as a distraction. Try playing first with the sound on. Your wife may get so pissed off with the clicks and beeps and that "Charge!" jingle whenever you score that she'll prefer that you channel surf. If she stands her ground, play with the sound off.

4. *We are not men, without TiVO:* True salvation lies in the most revolutionary television technology since the remote control itself. TiVO radically alters the way you can watch television, taking much of the pressure off of the obsessed clicker. Just relax, take a deep breath, and visualize watching everything you want, when you decide and at your own pace. These are truly magical times in which we live.

How to Get out of Bed Without Waking Her

You've seen the movie *Tremors,* right? Your sleeping wife is just like one of those "graboids" or "snake-oids" or whatever. The surface is calm, but just below slithers a raging, insatiable serpent, bent on dragging you down to a gruesome demise. With the slightest vibration, the beast emerges, its hideous maw agape in a blind search for prey. I'm still taking about the movie here, in case you weren't sure.

Fortunately, as with the graboids, the sleeping wife is predictable, and can therefore be thwarted. Here's how:

When You Get Up, Get Out

There's no greater mistake a husband can make than breaching consciousness and then hanging around. You get a little fidgety and start feeling rambunctious. You entertain thoughts of Dutch ovens and wet willies. You poor, unsuspecting bastard. Remember what happened to old Fred in *Tremors?* He never knew what hit him, but it wasn't coyotes, and that's for damn sure.

Go Gently into the Dewy Morn

Do not, under any circumstances, fling anything, neither blankets from the bed nor undies from your bum. If you're on the left side of the bed, slowly reach across with your right arm and grab the corner of the blankets. Gently bring your arm back across and down to your right side, thus sealing your wife in on her side of the bed. Now, slide your left leg off the bed, and place your left foot on the floor. Follow with your right leg. Bring yourself to a standing position, or better yet, hit the floor and crawl away on your belly.

Go Away, Go Far Away

The graboids sensed vibrations in the ground. Your wife, unfortunately, has much more sophisticated sensory apparatus at her disposal. In particular, be sure she's clear of the blast radius before emitting any gaseous eruptions. Most women can be convinced to forgive if they're awakened by a double latte or a foot massage. Last night's pepperoni pizza is a different story altogether.

How to Put the Toilet Seat Down

Difficulty

T T

Reward

♥ ♥ ♥ ♥

As with so many maladies that make no sense at all to men, the first step to recovery is admitting that she's convinced you have a problem. Arguing over "the Toilet Seat Question" is a losing battle. No matter how many times you explain your side—if you have to put the seat up before you pee, it's not too much to ask that she put it down—you'll never win. Your best bet here is appeasement, like Chamberlain giving up Czechoslovakia, so start training yourself to do the right thing.

Of course, you could just pee sitting down, but that wouldn't be the manly thing to do, now would it? So, as usual, we'll do things the hard way and preserve some fleeting sense of matrimonial manhood.

Leaving the toilet seat down is a behavior you have to habituate yourself to, so we'll rely on the principles of behavioral psychology to get it done. Like the white rat or the pigeon, the husband (*Lovehandlus hairibackus*) will respond to positive or negative stimuli to either elicit or suppress certain behaviors. The use of rewards or punishments to shape behavior is called "operant conditioning," and was first proposed by B. F. Skinner in the 1930s.

Here's how it works:

1. First, print copies of some positive image (Pamela Anderson, a full rack of baby-back ribs, or a fifty-inch plasma-screen television with high definition native pixel resolution and progressive scan converter), as well as a note that says, "Please put the seat down when you're done."

2. Next, tape the picture to the underside of the toilet lid at the top, so that it's covered when the seat is up. Tape the note to the wall behind the toilet at eye level.

3. When you have to go, without looking at the image on the toilet lid, lift the seat and do your business, reading the note along the way. Then, when you're done, put the seat down and reap your reward, the positive image.

4. After a few weeks, tell your wife to remove and replace the note and picture at random intervals (keep in mind she may "accidentally" misplace the Pamela Anderson picture and replace it with a photo from your wedding album). After a while she'll be able to remove them altogether.

How to De-stink the Bathroom

Three little words: Light a match. Just light it, let it burn for a second, and then blow it out. It's so simple. And yet, like the salmon returning home to spawn and die, the extinction of the dinosaurs, and the way asparagus makes your pee smell all weird, the causes of this phenomenon continue to elude the greatest minds of science. Well, at least I've always wondered about it. Until now. Dr. Charles Carlin, professor of chemistry at Carlton College, explains:

> De-stinking the bathroom with a match is accomplished largely by the production of SO_2 (sulfur dioxide) upon striking the match. Sulfur compounds have a disproportionately large effect on the nose. We tend to be quite sensitive to them even in small amounts in the atmosphere. Thus, a sudden influx of SO_2 is easily able to overwhelm other unattractive scents floating about in the usually relatively small volume of the typical bathroom.

This is the same reason why gas companies add a sulfur compound to the methane they pump into our houses. You see, methane is completely odorless, so without adding a smell to it, we'd never be aware of any gas leaks. So they add the compound butyl thiol, which the human nose can detect in very small amounts. "In fact," Dr. Carlin notes, "our noses are just about as clever at detecting this scent as some of the most sophisticated scientific instruments available for the same analytical task."

While we've got our minds in the toilet, here are a couple of other bathroom etiquette tips from my friend Michael Weiss: Whether you're in a crowded public bathroom, or the powder room at your in-laws', the primary potty faux pas is noise. So be sure to pee along the sides of the bowl above the waterline. And, if you've got to fart, create a "butt muffler" by using a wad of toilet paper as a mute to avoid any blatant blasts (see "How to Eliminate Gas," page 13, for other, more preventative measures).

How to Be Handy

Besides "You're unconscionably wealthy," there's probably no greater compliment a husband can get from his wife, her parents, or her friends than "You're really handy." It implies a rugged self-sufficiency, a wholesome, pious stoicism, and (I have to assume) a certain girth in the trousers. Regardless of whether any of those qualities apply to you, the more you're seen as handy, the more they'll seem to fit. Sounds like a worthwhile endeavor, eh?

Get to Know Your House

Just like a "car guy" can rattle off all the arcane technical details of his engine specs, the handy guy should know just about everything about his house. Take some time this weekend to really get to know its structure and inner workings. Do you know where your main water shutoff valve is? If you follow your water lines backward through your basement, you'll probably see a main line leaving the house with a large valve just before the wall. That's it. Test it just to be sure.

How about your circuit breaker panel? Do you know where it is, and are all the breakers labeled? Are your walls drywall or lath and plaster? Check behind a light switch. If you see a clean edge and uniform thickness, you've got drywall. If you see a choppy surface with some old, thin strips of wood behind, that's lath and plaster. How about your heating and hot water systems? Your roof? Your foundation? These are all things you should be familiar with. If you can't figure them out yourself, ask an experienced friend, or ask the next repairman you've got in the house. There's always something new to learn, but you've got to want to know and keep asking questions.

Be Informed

The handy husband isn't marked so much by what he knows how to do, but by how easily he teaches himself the things he doesn't. Let's face it, the only skills you need cluttering up that brain of yours are the ones you actually use. If you have never been faced with a leaky pipe or a loose floorboard, there's no reason to know how to fix them. But once this problem arises, the handy husband springs into action.

The first thing to do is make sure you've got a few good sources of information at your fingertips. You should own either *Home Improvement 1-2-3* from Home Depot or *The New Complete Do-It-Yourself Manual* from Reader's Digest, or some other comprehensive home maintenance guidebook. You should also consider getting a subscription to one of the many home maintenance magazines. My favorite is *Fine Homebuilding*, because it tends to stick to the fundamentals but produces superior results. Finally, figure out which friends or family members you can call for advice. These guys will be indispensable, since they've already learned from their mistakes and will be happy to share whatever tricks they've figured out so you can do things right the first time.

Now that you've got all these resources, you've got to actually use them. That means learning as much as you can about a new project before you begin. Sometimes, especially when an experienced friend says so, you should just forget it and hire a pro (see "How to Know Your Limitations," page 7). But for a great many household repair projects, you're the perfect guy for the job. Once you're comfortable with the steps involved, you can get started.

Get Organized

Before you begin any project, make sure you've got ample workspace dedicated to it. This can either be a permanent workshop, or just a makeshift setup with a table or drop cloth in the backyard. Give yourself lots of room, and make sure you've got a large, flat surface to work on and electricity nearby, if necessary. Finally, do an inventory to make sure you've got everything you'll need, especially the right tools.

Use the Right Tool for the Job

Nothing says "amateur" like using the wrong tool. It's inefficient, ineffective, and often dangerous. It's always worth the money to buy the right tool. For particularly expensive tools or tools with very limited use, ask around and see if you can borrow one from a friend, or rent one just for the time you'll need it. If you're lucky, the friend will volunteer to come along and do all the difficult parts himself. That reminds me—when you're out at the hardware store picking up all your supplies, stop on the way home and grab a case of beer as payment for any unexpected helpers.

Other Tools and Supplies

In addition to the basics (hammer, screwdrivers, pliers, et cetera) that every card-carrying member of the male gender should have, here are a few additional tools that you may not own but that will make all the difference as you learn how to be handy.

T Square: This is an indispensable tool for marking straight lines. Buy the largest one they've got; it should cost less than $20.

Level: You should probably have at least two levels, one large (at least three feet) and one small. Actually, these days you can get a really nifty laser level cheap. They're not quite as practical or easy to use, but that's far outweighed by the coolness factor.

Voltmeter: If you're even thinking about fiddling with anything electrical, you've got to have a voltmeter. Even the pros are never convinced a line is dead until they prove it. Then, and only then, should you consider handling electrical wiring.

Pocket hole jig: This is one you may have never even heard of. A pockethole joint consists of a hole drilled at an angle in one piece of wood, directed toward the piece to which it will be attached. The two pieces are attached with a screw driven down the hole and into the other piece. The Kreg Tool Company makes a pockethole jig that I promise will be one of your favorite tools. It's simple, cheap, and it works.

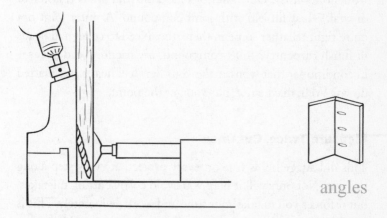

angles

Clamps: Clamps always seem like one of those luxury tools that only the pros should have. The fact is, everyone should have a decent set of clamps. Next time you're out at the hardware store, pick up a couple of small, medium, and large clamps. They're not that expensive, and you'll get more use out of them than you ever imagined.

Plumber's putty and pipe joint compound: Most leaking pipes and drains can be fixed with pipe joint compound or plumber's putty. If a joint between two threaded pipes is leaking, try putting some joint compound around the first three threads. Plumber's putty is a nonhardening oil-based product that is molded into a thin rope and used to seat gaskets and flanges in sinks and toilets. Some plumbers recommend forgoing plumber's putty and using silicone caulk as an alternative sealant.

Joint compound: Handymen just love joint compound. It's dirt cheap, comes in a big-ass bucket (get the Sheetrock All Purpose Joint Compound in the green bucket, which is easy to work with and less likely to crack than other brands), cleans up easily, and works on just about everything. It's like the duct tape of hole and crack repair (except joint compound actually works on joints). Got holes or cracks in your walls (plaster or drywall)? Just fill 'em with joint compound. A miter joint not quite right? Slather some in there, too. Need to cover nail heads in finish carpentry? Joint compound, my friend. Need a leave-in conditioner that won't make your hair feel heavy and matted down? Well, maybe not, but you get the point.

Measure Twice, Cut Once

This old adage holds true on every project, at every step along the way. Not only will it help you avoid costly cutting mistakes, but it forces you to take your time and work deliberately. This is particularly important as you begin to get comfortable with a project. At the beginning, you'll be very careful since you don't really know what you're doing. It's when you think you know what you're doing that you're most likely to get hasty and make mistakes. So just when you feel like you can do no wrong, that's precisely when you will, and precisely when you should be most careful.

Stay Organized

One of the most important tools to keep at your disposal is also the smallest and the cheapest: a good sharp pencil. If you're constantly losing your pencil, your workspace is too disorganized. I'm not talking about clutter—each person has his own ways of organizing a mess. But if you can't find your pencil quickly every time you need it, it's time to think about cleaning up (or at least reorganizing) your workspace.

Your First New Project

I can't just leave you with all this new information and not suggest a good way to put it all to use. So here's a great project to establish your status as the ultimate handy husband. It involves many of the tips, techniques, and tools we've just talked about, it'll save you a ton of money compared with what the professionals charge, and it's something that your wife will really appreciate: framing and hanging artwork.

Framing is really important for preserving your favorite works of art (even cheap posters can look great in a nice frame) and creating a stylish interior design. But as I'm sure you know, professional framing is incredibly expensive. So why not do it yourself? You're a handy guy, after all.

First, measure the dimensions of your artwork carefully (measure at least twice). If you need to trim the artwork at all, use your T square and an X-Acto knife to get a clean edge (always leave at least an inch or so of border on all sides of the artwork).

Go to www.americanframe.com and select your frame, plexiglass, matting, and backing. They'll walk you through the entire process and send you everything you'll need, cut perfectly to size. Their customer service is great and will answer any questions you have. It's easy to assemble the frame, and then you're ready for hanging. Best of all, the whole thing will cost you less than half what a pro shop charges.

To hang your painting, be sure to use one of those special hanging hooks (American Frame will send you a few with your order). Mark the wall with a pencil. If you've got drywall, just drive the nail through the hanging hook down at an angle until it's secure. With lath and plaster, place an X of clear tape over your mark to prevent cracking, then gently tap the nail in. If the nail gets stuck, don't force it. It's hitting the lath, and forcing it might break the lath underneath. Remove the nail and drill a very small hole down at the same angle. Replace the nail and you should be all set.

If you want to be particularly anal about it, whip out your level and make sure your artwork is always perfectly straight. Now, whenever anyone comes by and comments on your beautiful artwork, you can tell them all about how you framed it yourself and saved a ton of money. They'll tell your wife how lucky she is to be married to such a great guy, and then turn to you. "You're so handy," they'll say with a smile, subconsciously checking your crotch.

How to Do the Grocery Shopping

I've got some bad news for you, fellas. All these years you've figured that grocery shopping was your wife's job. You're the hunter, she's the gatherer, right? Wrong. That evolutionary biology crap might be good in theory, but it never quite works in practice. For example, you might be biologically predisposed to mate with multiple partners, but does that mean you're getting lots of hot action on the side? I didn't think so.

Let's face it, you're no hunter, at least not in the "beat a mastodon to death with a big stick" sort of way. I'm sorry to say, but in this modern, domestic world of pudgy men in khakis and boat shoes, grocery shopping is about as close to subsistence hunting as you're going to get. (Ever try to get past the little old ladies and grab a box of bran cereal on a Friday afternoon? Now *that's* survival of the fittest.) So rather than fight your innate urge to explore the wilds of the modern grocery store, you should embrace your inner shopper, since he represents the last lingering vestige of your inner caveman. Of course, if you screw it up, don't be surprised if your wife reacts in a "beat the crap out of my idiot husband with a big stick" sort of way. Here are some suggestions to help guarantee a successful hunt.

1. *Always work from a list:* Ideally, have your wife make the list (and thus accept the ultimate blame). The goal here is to distance yourself as far from any real responsibility in this process as possible. Once you enter the melee of the market, you'll be lucky if you can remember anything beyond "a loaf of

bread, a quart of milk, and a stick of butter." If you have to make the list, be sure to check current inventory first. Buying a duplicate of something is almost as bad as forgetting to buy something you genuinely need. Finally, since men are more visually oriented, you may even want to create a list that includes pictures of the particular products.

2. *Get specific:* Ask your wife if there are certain brands that she must have. If she doesn't specify a brand, then just buy an inexpensive one, whether it's a generic or a name brand on sale. By the way, don't just go by the price to determine which is cheapest. You've got to check the unit price. When a price is posted on the shelf, it usually says how much the item costs per ounce or per pound. Check that cost to figure out which is least expensive.

3. *Navigate the maze:* Don't use products at the ends of aisles as indicators of what's farther down the aisle. There's usually no connection whatsoever. The signs hanging above the aisle are your only indicator of what's down each one. Also, if you're looking for bargains, try the "squat and stretch" method of looking down low or up high. Those less desirable product placements tend to harbor better deals.

4. *Home field advantage:* Always shop at the same store your wife uses. She'll be familiar with what products they carry. If you go somewhere else, it's pretty much a guarantee that they'll be out of the one item she really needs.

5. *Don't shop hungry:* Always eat before you shop. Otherwise, you'll come home with nothing but Pringles and Ho Hos.

6. *Timing is everything:* If you want to beat the crowds, the best times to go shopping are usually very early or very late. Late afternoons are usually bad, and weekends will be the worst.

7. *Stay connected:* Always bring a cell phone with you when you go shopping. If you're feeling faint, or something is out of stock, you can call the wife for support.

8. *The produce problem:* Picking good fruit and vegetables can be tough. As a general rule, look for brightly colored produce that smells fresh. It's broken down into two classes, the firm and the forgiving. Firm produce, like broccoli, peppers, apples, potatoes, and so on, should feel solid with no soft spots. Forgiving produce, like tomatoes, citrus fruits, bananas, and the like, should give a little when squeezed but still feel solid. And just so you know, a cantaloupe is ripe when it has a strong sweet aroma, a golden color underneath the "webbing" on the rind, and a soft but not squishy stem end.

9. *The checkout challenge:* Selecting the best checkout line is the key to the entire shopping experience. Keep in mind that the shortest line is not always the best. You don't want to get stuck behind people who are distracted or confused, who demand to find the exact change buried deep inside their purses, or who pay by check. That usually means avoiding lines with old ladies, women rooting through their purses, or anyone with children in tow. You're ideally looking for a line with single people, mostly men. In particular, look for people who've already got their debit cards out. Finally, use the express line whenever possible. Keep in mind that multiples are combined together, so a dozen donuts only counts as one item (finally).

10. *Point-of-purchase protocol:* While you're waiting in line, avoid long, leering stares at the hot chicks on all the women's magazines. And keep in mind, if you suddenly find yourself overcome with dread over aliens infiltrating the Defense Department, homeless mutant zombies, or giant killer babies, you may want to confirm those stories by checking sources more credible than *The Weekly World News.*

How to Wash the Windows

Difficulty
T T T T

Reward
♥ ♥ ♥ ♥

This may just be propaganda from the Society of Overworked and Underaroused Housewives, but Dr. John Gottman of the University of Washington recently found that husbands who do housework are more sexually attractive to their wives. Another study found that men who did housework enjoyed sex with their wives more than those who didn't. And how about this: Sociologists at the University of California, Riverside, found that children who did housework with their fathers had more friends and were less depressed. So don't just clean the house so it's clean. Think of the little ones! Or consider house cleaning as just another in that seemingly infinite list of things you'll do to get some action.

Regardless of why you're doing it, participating in house cleaning is an essential trait of the perfect husband. And the one task that will earn you the most brownie points in her book is washing the windows.

Over the years your windows have become so encrusted with silt and other muck that even on a bright, sunny Saturday it feels like you live on the *Blade Runner* set. So you grab a bottle of window cleaner and a roll of paper towels. One or two streaky, still-grimy windows later you collapse on the couch in a heap of exhaustion and Heinekens. Sound familiar? Well, washing the windows shouldn't be such a miserable experience, and your results needn't be anything less than perfectly clean, streak-free windows.

First of all, you've probably overlooked the huge upside in all that wifely nagging: carte blanche at the janitorial supply store! What's that, you say? You've never been to one of these manly meccas of maintenance? Well, my friend, you're in for a treat. Imagine aisle upon aisle of industrial strength chemicals, multiscented urinal cakes, and innumerable implements of domestic destruction. Once you've discovered the janitorial supply store, your wife will rue the day she asked you to wash the windows. Let's face it, when it comes to doing chores like window washing, a garage full of useless gadgets and cool chemicals is the best revenge.

So head over to the supply store, tell them your tale of woe, and they'll set you up with everything you need. If you don't feel like asking for assistance, just pick up a squeegee, a scrubber with a handle (the coolest one comes with a holster-bucket so you can wear it on your belt), window washing fluid, and the kind of super-absorbent rag that soaks up so much fluid you may want to use it as a drop cloth in the living room on NFL Sundays. If they've got a tool belt that you can hang everything on, that'd look really cool in a retro-Schneider sort of way. Also, if you've got a multistory house, you may want to consider getting extension poles so you don't have to climb up too high to get at the windows. Finally, if you ever needed an excuse to buy a bright orange jumpsuit, this is it. Pete Townshend, eat your heart out.

Now it's time to get started with the task at hand. First off, determine if you've got the kind of windows that tilt inside. Look on either side of the window lock. If you see two finger holes with spring-loaded buttons, you're golden. Unlock the window and open it a bit, press the two buttons toward the center, and the whole frame should tilt inward. You can slide down the top frame as well and do the same thing. This will make the entire process much easier.

If you have conventional windows, remove all the screens

(and storm windows, if you have them) before you get started. When you're done with the windows, you can wash the screens by soaking the scrubber and working it over both sides of each screen. Then just let them air dry.

There's a simple technique for washing windows, but each step is essential to guarantee clear, streakless panes. First of all, don't wash the windows in direct sunlight, because the solution will dry too quickly and cause streaking. Either wait for a cloudy day or work around the house, always staying in the shade. To get started, soak your scrubber in washing solution, and scrub the entire window to loosen up all the dirt. If you don't have washing liquid, you can add a half cup of white vinegar and a half cup of ammonia to a gallon of warm water. Next, use the drying cloth to wipe a dry strip across the top of the window. Making sure the squeegee is dry, place it in the dry

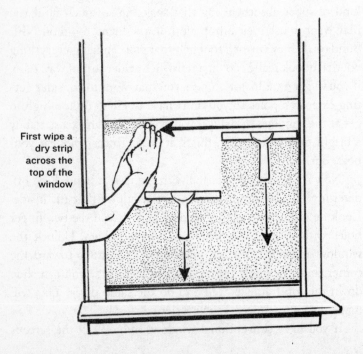

First wipe a dry strip across the top of the window

strip at the top and drag it down to the bottom. Wipe the squeegee dry and repeat across the window. Finally, use the cloth to wipe the sides and bottom of the window frame.

You'll be done before you know it, and while you may not be completely exhausted, a house full of clean windows is a good enough excuse to collapse on the couch beneath a heap of Heinekens.

How to Be Prepared in a Blackout

While it may be perfectly acceptable these days for your wife to earn more money than you, cook less frequently than you, and in some cases even bench press more than you, blackout preparedness remains firmly in the husbandly domain. So, take this opportunity to play '50s sitcom dad, throw on a pair of leisure slacks and a plaid shirt, and get ready to protect your family the way every red-blooded American family man should.

Unlike gift buying, dishwashing, or "it" doing, when it comes to being prepared in a blackout (or any number of other disasters, for that matter), more is not necessarily better. There are some basic things you should do to protect your family, but when you start drawing up plans for a bomb shelter and begin stockpiling weapons, you may draw some curious glances from your wife, the neighbors, and the local authorities. So, rather than following the Boy Scout motto, "Be Prepared," we'll follow the complacent husband's motto, "Be Prepared Enough."

The Basics

I'll bet you've got a flashlight somewhere. Take a moment, while the lights are still on, to find it. I'll also bet the batteries are dead, or it doesn't even have batteries. Take this moment, before the looting and price gouging begin, to buy new batteries and put them in the flashlight. Now, put it somewhere so you can find it in the dark, like a kitchen drawer or the front closet.

Next, set aside some space in the garage or basement to store your emergency supplies.

Matches: Don't take the matches from the bathroom—those are already providing a vital public service.

Radio: Keep a battery-operated radio on hand. As with the flashlight, this device functions suboptimally with dead or missing batteries.

Water: Store a three-day supply of water (at least one gallon per person per day). You may also want to keep some empty bottles on hand. These can be filled immediately after a power outage to supplement your supply. Remember, in an absolute emergency, you can get water from the hot-water heater, the toilet tank (not the bowl), or from melting ice cubes.

Food: You should also have a three-day supply of nonperishable food on hand. This is just a precaution, since the food in your refrigerator will be fine for a while, and the food in the freezer should hold for up to three days. To keep perishables cold as long as possible, avoid opening the refrigerator or freezer doors any more frequently than necessary.

Money: In case the ATMs go down, keep a stash of cash with your emergency supplies. Keep in mind the local convenience store will be charging $14 a bagel, so you may want to tuck away a bit more than you first thought. Just make sure to remember where you stash it.

Telephones: Keep your cell phones charged, and keep an old phone that doesn't need to be plugged in. Cell phone service may be down in a blackout, but you should still be able to use a nonelectric phone.

Get Your Fill

If you've got critical medications that you must take on a regular basis, make sure you don't let your prescription run out before getting a refill. Always have at least a week's worth of medication on hand. Also, you may want to get in the habit of keeping at least a half tank of gas in your car.

Contingency Plans

Be sure to have a plan if your family is separated during a blackout. Establish a meet-up place for everyone, as well as contingencies in case people cannot get there. Your children's school will have an emergency plan, so make sure you know what that is. Arrange to have a neighbor or friend pick up the kids if you are unable to. Also, have a plan for getting home from work if your normal routine is interrupted, and establish a place to go if you cannot get home from work.

Let There Be Light

Don't forget, the power will come back on someday. So, to avoid a potentially damaging power surge, remember to turn off your computer, television, stereo, and other electronic equipment.

Note: Many of the recommendations above are based on a recent Family Preparedness Planning report from the National Center for Disaster Preparedness at Columbia University's Mailman School of Public Health. For additional information on disaster preparedness, visit the Red Cross website at www. redcross.org.

How to Solder a Pipe

Difficulty
T T T
Reward
♥ ♥ ♥

Plumbing is such a manly activity—it involves metal, fire, and even something called flux (no, it's not some sort of smoked salmon fetish)—it's amazing how few husbands know how to do it. Mastering the craft will also keep the wife happy, especially after she finds out what the pros charge.

There are several kinds of pipe products and problems you may face, but the most mysterious and cost-efficient procedure seems to be soldering copper pipe, so that's what we'll deal with.

What You'll Need

> Propane torch
> Spark lighter
> Tubing cutter
> Wire brush for inside and outside of pipe
> Lead-free flux
> Flux brush
> Lead-free solder

Step I: Assess the Situation

If you've got a broken main, and your own private riptide in the basement, seek professional help immediately. But if you want to install a new outdoor spigot or fix a dripping joint, you're just the man for the job. However, you may want to reread the chapter on "How to Know Your Limitations" (page 7).

Step 2: Locate the Main Water Shutoff and Turn Off the Water

There are several ways of testing whether the water is actually off, but one is particularly entertaining: While your wife is taking her leisurely Sunday morning shower, head down to the basement and crank the main water valve closed. If you hear screaming, you know you've done it right (just be prepared to plead ignorance when eventually confronted—see "How to Apologize Convincingly," page 35).

Step 3: Measure and Cut the Pipe

When adding a new line perpendicular to an existing line, measure the distance from the current pipe to the end location. Insert the pipe into the tubing cutter and tighten the handle. Rotate the cutter once around the pipe, then once in the opposite direction. Continue to tighten the cutter every few rotations until you complete the cut.

Step 4: Prepare the Pipe

All connecting surfaces must be clean and dry. If you're cutting into an active line, it may be hard to dry it completely. Try stuffing a wad of white bread in there to dry it out. Then, when you're soldering, the room will fill with the pleasant aroma of toasting bread. When you're done, the water pressure will clean out the burnt bread crumbs. Thoroughly scuff the outside of the pipe ends and the inside of all connecting joints with the wire brush. Apply a healthy layer of flux to all connecting surfaces.

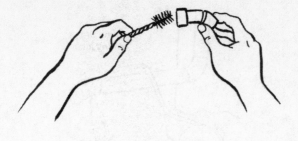

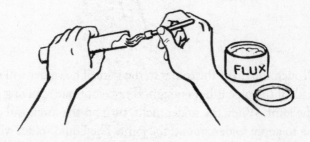

Step 5: Soldering the Pipe

Connect the pipes and the connectors. Twist the pipe in the joint to spread the flux throughout the joint. Unroll a few inches of solder and keep it handy. Light the torch by opening the valve and holding a flame at the end of the nozzle. Adjust the torch until the interior blue flame is about two inches long. If there is any flammable structure behind the pipe, be sure to use a heat shield to block the flame.

Apply the blue tip of the flame to the middle of the joint for several seconds. The flux will sizzle and smoke. Apply heat to the other side of the pipe for even distribution. Be careful, as copper is a great heat conductor and the entire length of pipe will get very hot.

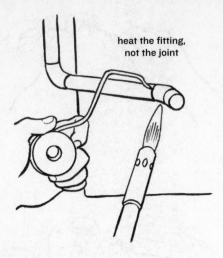

heat the fitting,
not the joint

Touch the tip of the solder to the joint. The solder will melt quickly if the pipe is hot enough. If not, continue applying heat to the joint. When the solder melts, turn off the torch and continue to apply solder around the joint. The liquid solder will be drawn into the joint. Apply solder until you get a thin line of solder all around the joint. Let the pipe cool, and then use a dry rag to wipe the joint clean. Finally, be sure to turn the water back on and test the joint before you even think about telling your wife what you've done.

How to Get Rid of Bugs

Unless your wife is the love-child of Ted Nugent and Leona Helmsley, she's probably not crazy about killing any kind of critter, even spiders and cockroaches. That's where you come in (of course). I don't know where women get the notion that men have either the wits or the cojones to handle this task, but it always seems to be our job. And since we've been charged with this task as men, we must approach and fulfill our duties as men—with as little effort as is humanly possible.

When it comes to bugs, too much information can be a dangerous thing. For instance, once you learn that a crushed bee can emit an odor signaling other bees to attack, or the whole thing about headless cockroaches living on for weeks, you may not only find it more difficult to kill them, but you may find yourself wanting to bow down before your new carapace-covered overlords. Or you may become so obsessed with killing all the vermin on your property that you overlook the many beneficial services that these bugs provide. To help you remain focused, we'll keep it simple, and just provide some basic suggestions to help you keep your house bug-free.

Ants

These guys aren't too gross, but there're just so many of them. You'll want to clean up whatever ants are around, cut off the incoming stream, and prevent future invasions. Odds are the ants you see are going after some food or water in your kitchen. You'll probably see the point where they're entering, and then a two-lane freeway of ants straight to and from the food or water. Leaving the food source there for now, just spray the ants with a soapy cleaner and wipe them away (you'll also wipe away the scent trail they've been following). Seal up the entry point with caulk (for caulking tips, see "How to Paint a Room," page 134). If you can't find an exact entry point, just place ant bait where the line of ants first appeared. When the ants are no longer around, remove the bait so you don't attract more into your house. To keep ants out, be sure to seal up cracks or other potential entry points with caulk, and keep your food in tightly sealed containers.

Spiders

Unless you're seriously arachnophobic, it's hard not to appreciate spiders. Their silk is super strong (about twice as strong as steel, by weight), a single web can contain sixty meters of silk, and spiders have eight eyes and forty-eight knees. But most important, spiders eat other bugs, so they're good to have around. Of course, you probably don't want them in your house, so here's a way to get rid of them without killing them. Keep a plastic cup and piece of thick paper around. Simply cover the spider with the cup, then slide the paper underneath to seal it inside. Take your "spider trap" outside and release the spider, where it can go on happily hunting insects.

Cockroaches

These guys are just nasty. You've got to get rid of them fast, and then prevent any others from showing up later. Here's a useful trick for catching cockroaches. Since these little buggers are extremely sensitive to the movement of air, it's very difficult to sneak up on them. The best way to get them is to use a vacuum cleaner with a hose attachment and suck them right up, and then throw the vacuum cleaner bag away. Then you'll need to take regular preventative measures, like keeping food in tightly sealed containers, sealing up baseboards and cupboards, minimizing clutter around your house, and eliminating leaky pipes (see "How to Solder a Pipe," page 113) and other water sources. You could set traps for them, but those aren't such a good idea if you've got kids or pets.

Bees

The occasional bee in the house shouldn't be a problem, but when you've got regular sightings in and around your home, it's time to take action. If there's a particular bee you want to get rid of, you can use your "spider trap" (see opposite) to capture it, and then either put the trap in the freezer to kill the bee, or release it back outside. If you've got flowers or a garden out there, you should release the bee, since that little guy's pollinating makes all the difference. If you've got lots of bees around, first make sure all obvious entry points are sealed off. Check your window screens, and make sure you've got screens over your attic vents. You should also seal off any cracks in your foundation, around windows, or anywhere else bees might get in.

Next, look around for an obvious nest. Bees can build external nests in eaves or under porches, or they can build in walls or other openings. Look for bees hovering around or climbing into cracks or holes to locate the nest. You might find a little pile of sawdust underneath a hole where carpenter bees have nested. To destroy the nest, wait until evening, when the bees will all be inside and calm. Then spray directly into the nest with bee or wasp killer, and run like hell. After the spray has dried, seal the hole with wood filler or caulk.

If you've got bees that have nested in the ground, forget what you've heard about pouring gasoline down there and setting the nest ablaze. No matter how much fun it may sound like, just hire a pro to take care of that.

How to Grow the Perfect Lawn

Difficulty

T T T T

Reward

♥ ♥

All men are inexorably drawn to the lawn. We can't resist its siren song, and yet few of us understand why. It's really just another household chore we should try to weasel our way out of, and a heavily labor-intensive and frustrating chore at that. And yet we forgo that Saturday morning tee time and that weekend fishing trip to stay home and babysit tens of thousands of three-inch high plants that don't even do anything cool like eat flies or meat. They just sit there motionless, gloating like an army of victorious Lilliputians. And yet we don't resist, and we work tirelessly for their cause.

Warren Schultz has developed a theory of why men are obsessed with their lawns. Schultz, a renowned lawn-care expert and author of *A Man's Turf: The Perfect Lawn,* breaks his theory down into seven parts.

1. *Domination:* Lawn maintenance is one of the few remaining opportunities for modern man to tame nature. Chopping the tops off thousands of plants is man's way of establishing who's in charge.
2. *Territoriality:* The lawn defines our domain. "The democratic spirit is to open our land to others," Schultz writes, "but we still need to mark our space."
3. *Belonging:* Our universal commitment to our lawns is an unwritten bond between men.
4. *Play:* The lawn is where the inner child can run free. It's one of the few remaining places where men can truly be boys.

5. *Nature:* Our bond with nature is primordial, and we find ourselves tied to the natural rhythms of the grass.
6. *Safety:* Clearing the land has always been a good defense against surprise ambush. While today we may only need to keep a lookout for nosy neighbors, it's the same principle.
7. *Privilege:* Schultz captures this one perfectly: "A man's lawn is his welcome mat, the first impression he gives about how he lives his life, an emblem of his wealth and position."

So, now that you know why you're obsessed with your lawn, you'll need to know how to keep it looking beautiful.

Go Long

You might prefer your lawn cut short enough for putting practice, but unless you've got the right kind of grass you're probably cutting the plants way too short for their own good. Most grasses should be grown longer, about three inches, which helps the plants retain water and can shade out weeds and prevent them from growing. Definitely find out what kind of grass you've got, and ask how tall the plants should grow before cutting.

Cutting at Night

The best time to cut is in the evenings. This gives the plants as much time as possible to recover before they have to face the heat of the next day's sun.

Just a Little Trim

Regardless of the height of your grass, never cut off more than one-third of the blade while mowing. Cutting the grass any shorter will overly stress the plant. Also, that top third of the blade is almost all water, so it will decompose easily and naturally fertilize the remaining grass plant.

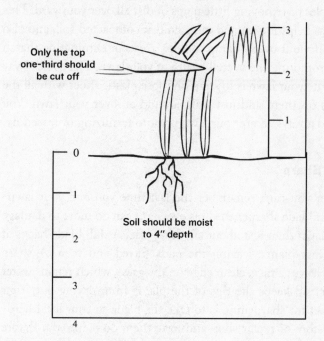

Only the top one-third should be cut off

Soil should be moist to 4" depth

Avoid the Thatch

If you follow the rule of one-third, then you shouldn't need to rake or sweep your lawn of the grass clippings. The cut grass will break down and act as a natural fertilizer. These clippings should not contribute to thatch buildup on your lawn, which is caused by dead plants and roots that don't decompose and form a thick weave between the grass and the soil, preventing enough water, air, and nutrients from getting down to the roots. If your thatch gets more than about a half inch thick, you can remove it with a rake.

Aerate

If your lawn is more than even just a couple years old, you should probably be aerating it annually. Aeration involves poking holes or removing little plugs of dirt all over your yard. This process helps loosen and moisten dry, compacted soil, and also helps dry out overly damp soil. It's great for eliminating thatch and promoting the overall health of your lawn. The coolest way to aerate your lawn is to strap on those plastic shoes with all the spikes on them and just walk around all over your lawn. You should always aerate your lawn prior to fertilizing or reseeding.

Stay Sharp

I'll bet you can't remember the last time you had your lawn-mower blade sharpened. This oversight can do more to damage your lawn than just about anything else. A dull blade hacks at the grass plants, leaving the ends frayed and torn. A sharp blade leaves a nice, clean edge on the grass, which retains water better and keeps the tips of the plants from drying out. Your best bet for sharpening is to take the blade to your local hardware store or repair shop and have them do it for you. Before removing the blade, first disconnect the spark-plug wire to make sure your mower doesn't start up accidentally. Lock the blade in place against a piece of wood stuck through the grass chute. Use a little penetrating oil or WD-40 if the bolt won't budge.

Water Wise

There are many myths and misconceptions about when, how much, and how often to water your lawn. Here are some basic guidelines to help you keep your lawn in great shape: You should water the lawn either in the early morning or the early evening, so the water won't evaporate too quickly from the heat. Most lawns need about one inch of water a week, which should be enough to soak down about four inches into the soil. You can fine-tune this process by placing some small containers around your yard while watering. When the level reaches one inch, dig a shovel into the ground and see how deep the water has penetrated. If the moisture stays too shallow or goes too deep, adjust your watering time accordingly. If any puddles form while you're watering, stop and let all the water soak in. As a rule, less water is always better than more.

Reseeding

Grass plants thrive in the cooler weather of the spring and fall. Therefore, those are the best times to reseed your lawn (known as "overseeding"). If you're filling in bare patches, rake over the dirt to remove any debris and loosen the soil. Sprinkle the seeds over the soil, cover with a thin layer of top soil or seeding mulch, and water gently and regularly until the new plants appear.

Fertilizer

Fertilizing can be tricky. If you don't use enough, your lawn can be thin and bland. Too much fertilizer can promote thatch growth and other problems. So always consult a lawn-care expert in your area for specific advice. In general, you want a fertilizer that will take care of both the grass plant and the soil. Grass plants thrive on nitrogen, which promotes healthy, green leaves, so make sure your fertilizer contains some controlled-release nitrogen. You also want a fertilizer that promotes the development of humus, the rich organic top soil that promotes healthy grass. You'll probably want to fertilize in the spring, but you definitely want to fertilize in the fall, when grass plants prepare themselves for dormancy and next year's growing season.

How to Iron Your Own Damn Shirt

Difficulty

T T

Reward

♥ ♥

There are many instances in which your ineptitude is an asset, prompting your wife to step in and finish the chores you're incapable of doing correctly. This, my friend, is not one of them. Imagine this scenario: Because she had to iron your shirt, your wife takes even longer to get ready to leave for the evening. What's worse is that she has a valid excuse for her tardiness. And worst of all, said excuse names you as the sole defendant. So rather than make a bad situation much, much, much worse, let's try to make the best of a bad thing.

I'd suggest just taking your shirts to the nearest dry cleaners, but I assume if you're reading this you just got back from the golf course or the basement and you've got forty-five minutes to clean yourself up, get dressed, and get out the door. I'd ask why you didn't think to drop your shirts off well ahead of time, but I'm sure you've been asked that question several times in the past ten minutes, and by someone you find a lot more intimidating than me. Since you didn't have a good answer for your wife, why should I expect anything different?

Despite what you may now be contemplating, relying on your gut to stretch out the fabric sufficiently to remove any wrinkles is not a viable strategy at this point. You've got work to do, but it's not that bad.

Grab your dress shirt off the floor in your closet or from the backseat of your car, put it on a wooden hanger, and hang it in the bathroom before you shower. Button one of the top buttons to keep the shirt on the hanger so you don't end up accidentally using it as a bath mat. The steam will loosen up the fibers and do much of the work for you. This method will not get the job done completely. You may not agree; your wife most certainly will.

After you've gotten yourself shaved, coiffed, and almost fully dressed, you can iron your shirt. This way, all the blood on your face will have a chance to dry, and won't end up on your collar. Now ask your wife where she keeps the iron and the ironing board. After she regains consciousness, note that setting up an ironing board is trickier than you'd think. The collapsible legs are released by a little latch underneath toward the front. Slide that latch to the side, and you should be able to lower the legs. Set up the ironing board near an outlet.

It's easiest to iron a shirt when it's a little damp. Forget about using the steam function on the iron, which will only spit and gurgle, then dribble little puddles of water at your feet. Grab one of those little plastic spray bottles, and fill it with warm water. While you're ironing, lightly spray the shirt with a very fine mist of water. To determine which heat setting to use, check the tag on your shirt (if it doesn't say mostly cotton, there's some clothes shopping in your future, young man) and set the iron temperature according to that fabric. Now, plug in the iron, set it upright on the ironing board, let it warm up, and you're good to go.

First, unbutton the shirt. If it has a button-down collar, unbutton that as well. Or if your shirt has those plastic collar stays in the collar, be sure to remove them. Open up the shirt and lay it over the ironing board, tag side down. Lift open the collar and, using only the first inch or so of the hot iron, press along the back of the collar from the points inward. Then turn the shirt over and iron the front of the collar. Close the collar and give a quick pass to press the collar seam.

Next, lay the shirt on its back with one sleeve out straight along the board. Flip the cuff inside out and iron it on both sides. Turn the cuff back out, and iron the entire sleeve from the shoulder down to the cuff. Repeat for the other sleeve.

Now, lay the shirt over the board so that half of the collar is on top of the narrow end of the board and one of the front halves of the shirt lies flat on the board surface. Use the entire iron surface to smooth the fabric. Be particularly careful around buttons and the shoulder. Then, rotate the shirt around the board so you can iron the back of the shirt. Continue rotating until you can iron the other front half.

That's it, you're done. Bet it didn't take as long as you thought. Of course, no matter how long it takes, you're still

going to end up waiting for her to get ready to leave. You could occupy yourself for a little while longer trying to figure out how to close up the damn ironing board again. Or see "How to Wait Patiently Until She's Ready to Leave" (page 187).

And, oh yeah, don't forget to unplug the iron before you leave.

How to Make the Bed

The question we must first answer is not "How do we make the bed?" but rather, "Why should we?" After all, in a little over twelve hours, you're just going to pull the covers down and muss it up all over again. This is a sentiment that Michael Gurian, in his book *What Could He Be Thinking?*, sees as indicative of the "hunter's" or "camper's" brain. The unmade bed just feels more natural for us. It's a great dilemma, I know, and one with no clear resolution. Except possibly this one: Just make the damn bed or your wife will be royally pissed!

The problem seems to stem from the fact that men see bed-making as a domestic task, and thus run screaming from it. After all, anything that involves linens, pillows, and poofy, paisley shams just doesn't seem like a manly endeavor. And while there may be fluffing involved, it's not the kind of fluffing that would get a guy's attention. So how can I convince the groggy, semiconscious husband, his boxers all drooping and his bedhead sticking out every which way, to conjure enough balance and coordination to reassemble the bed?

First, try thinking of bed-making as a furniture refinishing project, rather than a domestic chore. Granted, it's a project that needs refinishing every freaking day, but bear with me on this one. Sure, you're working with pillowcases and sheets rather than wood trim and finish nails, but making the bed is much like a construction project, with its geometry and tight seams. Imagine the bed as a piece of unfinished furniture, with you as the master craftsman putting on the finishing touches. It's a stretch, I know, but it may do the trick for you.

For those of you still resistant to the task, I've got a few friendly words of advice: "ATTENNNNNNN-HUT, MAG-GOT!!! You call that a bed, Private? Why, I've seen cleaner sheets crumpled up in my toilet! Listen up, Daisy May, if I can't bounce a quarter off that bed, I'll bounce it off your skull! And what's with that hair, Alice? Looks like Don King got his head stuck in a blender!"

That's right, soldier, hospital corners aren't just the province of nurses, they're also made by bad-ass drill sergeants, many of whom apparently had serious potty training issues as children. So if you don't want to have small change hurled at your face each morning, you'd better make your bed, and make it right. Here's how:

1. If you've got a fitted sheet, just put it on the mattress, pulling over two corners, then walk around to the other side and pull it on the other two corners.

2. If you've got a flat bottom sheet, place it over the mattress so there's an even overhang on all sides. Tuck one end under the head of the mattress. Then go to the foot, pull the sheet taut, and tuck it in as well.

3. To make hospital corners, start at the foot of the bed and grasp the sheet with both hands, one at the corner and the other about eight inches up along the side. Pull the corner of the sheet down and then sweep it toward the head of the bed and tuck it under the side of the mattress. Then drape the over-hanging flap down vertically and tuck it under the mattress, pulling it taut to make a vertical seam at the very corner of the mattress. Repeat this on all four corners and tuck the rest of both edges under the sides of the mattress.

4. For the top sheet, lay the sheet over the mattress, but make sure the short edge with the wide hem goes just to the edge of the mattress but doesn't hang over the head of the bed.

Tuck in the edge at the foot of the bed and make hospital corners at that end. Then, tuck in the sides, but leave about two feet untucked toward the head of the bed.

5. Lay the blanket on the bed, leaving enough room at the top for pillows. Tuck in the blanket the same way you did the top sheet. Then, fold the top sheet back down over the blanket and tuck the sides under the mattress.

6. If you've got a bedspread, throw it over the bed so it hangs evenly, then tuck it slightly under the pillows.

7. Now, hit the showers!

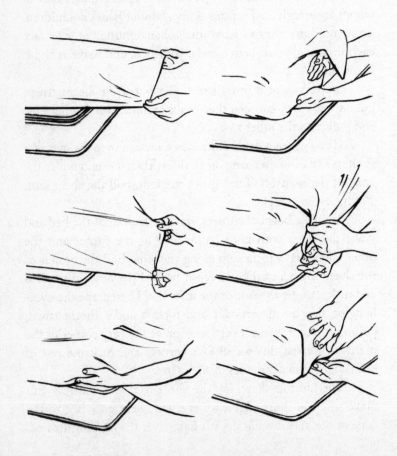

Of course, you could just get a duvet, pull it up over all the wrinkled sheets and everything, smooth it out, and call it done. Your wife won't notice anything until you get back into bed that night, and by then it's too late, and she's too tired to do anything about it. Yeah, I think that's the option I'd go for.

How to Paint a Room

Difficulty

T T T T

Reward

♥ ♥ ♥ ♥

When it comes to any talk of painting a room, your wife is a master of the rhetorical conversation. She'll say things like "Do you think we should paint the dining room?" Or "Which of these colors do you like best?" Or "Do you think we should hire somebody or can you handle this one yourself?" Now, she knows the answers to these questions, and you know that she knows. And yet, you're just a big enough schmuck to actually give her your honest opinion. As if that ever mattered. You're going to be painting that room, and you're going to paint it the color of her choosing. But by virtue of her asking your opinion, and your naive and futile attempts to participate in the design process, the blame will fall squarely on you if the color's not exactly perfect or it peels a few years down the road. Read the fine print in your marriage contract, buddy, it's all in there. So you had better do it right.

I used to paint houses during the summer in high school and college. I can safely mention this because I'm reasonably sure the statute of limitations has expired on any potential litigation. I learned a lot of great tricks and techniques over those years, and assuming that heat stroke, paint fumes, and caffeine addiction haven't completely compromised the associated brain matter, I'll attempt to share some of those tips with you.

Buying Supplies

There's a simple rule to follow when buying supplies: If in doubt, buy the more expensive item. Your goals here are to do the job right, but also to do it fast. Expensive brushes are so worth it. They hold more paint and give you cleaner edges and fewer brush lines. With proper care they'll also last much longer than cheap ones, so they'll prove to be a better deal in the long run. For a sure bet, buy a Purdy three-inch angled brush, available at most hardware stores.

Buy canvas drop cloths. Yes, they're much more expensive than the plastic, but they're worth it. They're much easier to work with, they get into corners and along edges much better, and they'll last longer.

Here's a rough list of what you'll need to paint a room:

Small paint bucket
Drop cloths
Paint brush
Caulk and caulking gun
Putty knives
Joint compound
Sandpaper
Roller tray
Roller handle
Roller pad

Selecting Clothes

Do not grab that hideous shirt she gave you for Christmas three years ago. I don't care if this will be the first and only time you wear it. Why make a bad day much, much worse? Ideally, you've got an old, tattered AC/DC shirt that she's always hated. If you can stand to part with it, this is a way to do it that will get her attention and garner some appreciation.

Choosing a Brand of Paint

As with your other supplies, there's a reason why some paints are more expensive than others: they're better. Higher quality paint has a higher volume of solids such as pigment and binder suspended in it. Pigment adds hardness and durability as well as color. Some paints list titanium dioxide as their type of pigment, but many add cheap extenders to their pigment such as silica and chalk (listed as calcium carbonate). Cheaper paints will also use acrylic compounds rather than 100 percent acrylic as their binder, which affects the gloss, adhesion, and color retention of the paint.

As far as the type and finish of paint, you probably want to use a latex paint rather oil-based, and you'll probably want a flat or eggshell finish on the walls and ceilings, with semigloss on the doors and trim.

Choosing Colors

Selecting colors can be a royal pain, but it's better to struggle with the decision up front rather than repaint the whole room afterward. I have a friend, Andrew, who has painted and repainted his dining room so many times, a cross section of his walls looks like the inside of a Gobstopper. Besides that, each new layer of paint diminishes the airspace to the point where there's hardly enough oxygen left in the room to keep the candles lit.

As I mentioned above, it is essential that your wife choose the color. Of course, you can't appear too deferential or she'll think you don't care. So, short of a Vulcan mind meld, the best you can do is hope to read the clues she's giving and figure out where she wants to go. She'll say something like, "How about this color, do you think it's too dark?" You can assume that she thinks it's too dark and counter with, "Yeah, I might go with something just a bit lighter." After dancing around like this for a week or so, she'll either tell you what she wants, or else she'll drop "the big one." You know the line: "I don't care, honey, whichever color you want is fine." That line is like Ezekiel 25:17 in *Pulp Fiction.* Once you hear it, your life is pretty much over.

Getting Ready

First you want to clear out the room as much as possible. If you're painting the ceiling, try to empty the room completely. If you're just doing the walls, gather everything into the middle of the room as compactly as possible. Remove all the switch plates and outlet covers, and keep all the covers and screws in a Ziploc bag for safekeeping. Take down any light fixtures (be sure the outlet is off, or better yet shut off the power to that circuit altogether), and remove any nails or other objects from the walls. And you may want to open the windows and get a fan going to avoid any unintended vapor-induced hallucinations.

Prepping the walls is by far the worst part of the job, and removing wallpaper is the worst type of prep. If you have wallpaper, and it's not just falling off the walls in sheets, I'd suggest hiring a professional. Trust me, it's worth the money.

The other prep you're likely to encounter is filling holes and cracks. Most holes and cracks on flat surfaces can be filled with spackle or joint compound. I find joint compound is easier to work with. Just use a small putty knife to scrape out any loose plaster around the hole, then fill it with joint compound and make a clean swipe with the knife to remove any excess. A good trick is to add just a little bit of tinted paint to the joint compound; that way, when it comes time to sand, you won't miss any spots.

For cracks along corners or around window frames, use caulk. You'll want to get a paintable interior caulk. Select a color that's close to your paint color. Cut the tip off the tube of caulk, place it into the caulking gun, and then squeeze out a line of caulk along the joint. For a perfectly smooth line, run a wet finger or a damp towel along the joint to remove any excess.

Let everything dry for at least a day, then sand down the joint compound until smooth and wipe off the wall with a barely damp cloth. Now you're ready to paint.

Painting the Walls

Painting is done in sequence from the highest point to the lowest. So we'll paint the walls from top to bottom, saving the trim for last. When painting any wall there are two things going on: cutting and rolling. Cutting is when you apply a thin strip of paint on the edge of wall, right where it meets up with a strip of molding, the ceiling, or a wall of another color. You may want to apply a strip of blue painter's masking tape on the adjacent wall to help you get a nice, straight line, but a steady hand and some subtly applied pressure is probably more efficient.

Learning to cut takes practice, so let's grab our brush and hold it against the wall so the tip of the bristles are just touching the surface. Now, press down, keeping the tip against the wall, and shift the brush handle sideways, still keeping the handle perpendicular to the wall. You'll notice that the tip of the brush will slide out in the other direction, and you'll get a nice sharp edge of bristles on the end. That's the edge that will give you a clean line of paint when you're cutting around a wall.

When you're ready to get started, mix the paint thoroughly and pour some into the small paint bucket about three inches deep. Start cutting at one corner of the wall: Paint a four- to six-inch wide horizontal strip about two feet over and a vertical strip four feet down. This area will be the first section you'll roll.

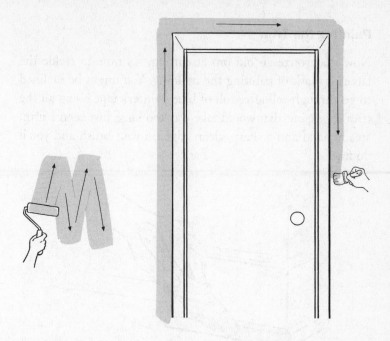

Rolling is the fun part, where you cover lots of ground in a little time. Pour your paint into the roller pan about halfway up. Push a roller pad onto the roller handle, and then roll it into the paint, drawing the handle back up onto the slanted part of the tray until you have paint evenly spread around the roller. When painting a ceiling or high wall, you may want to attach a threaded broom handle to the roller for easier extension.

Rolling technique is important in order to ensure an even coat with no lines. The easiest way to do it is to imagine rolling out a big *M* within that two-by-four-foot area. Begin with a smooth and slow upward stroke on the left side, then bring it down, curving to the right, then up again curving farther right, and then straight down. You can then use lighter vertical strokes, from top to bottom, to smooth out this area, and then repeat around the room.

Painting the Trim

Now that you're an old pro at cutting, it's time to tackle the laborious task of painting the molding. You might be inclined to go through roll after roll of blue painter's tape along all the trim edges, but that would take way too long. Just keep a firm, steady hand and a sharp, clean edge on your brush and you'll do fine.

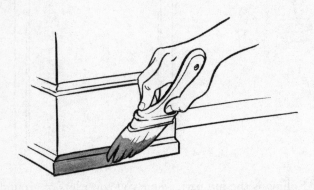

Cleanup

Before cleanup, be sure to pour any remaining paint in your paint pail or roller tray back into the paint can. Liquid latex paint is widely considered hazardous waste, although dry paint is not. So if you've got leftover paint, leave the lid off the can to let it dry completely and then throw it away with the regular trash. (Some towns have particular guidelines about tossing items like old paint—check with your local sanitation department.)

The most important part of cleanup is the brush. Clean your brush thoroughly in warm, soapy water. When you think it's good and clean, take it outside and "whip it" dry, as if you were winding up and throwing it straight into the ground (except don't let go). To test if it's actually clean, smack the bristles across your wrist. If you see any paint, it's not completely clean. Keep washing the brush until you can smack it across your wrist and just see clear water.

All that's left is a long, hot shower and a tall, cold beer.

How to Unclog the Bathroom Sink

If you're fortunate enough to have two sinks in your master bathroom, you'll very quickly discover the mixed blessing such a setup provides. On the plus side, her sink will definitely clog before yours. I don't care if you've got a ZZ Top–Sinead O'Connor thing going on, her sink will always slow first. The nice thing about this scenario is that it gives you free rein to blame her for all other plumbing-related problems throughout the house. The downside, of course, is that it's your job to do something about it. And fast.

The first thing you want to *not* do is call a plumber. Odds are you've got a basic clog, and a plumber will charge upward of $75 just for the honor of visiting your lovely abode, and desperately repress his gleeful giggle as the clock ticks away while he "works." We may eventually get to the point where you need professional assistance, but we're not there yet.

The next thing to *not* do is rush out and buy those liquid drain openers. I have never had any success with those, to the point where I think they should have a disclaimer on the bottle that says: "WARNING: THIS PRODUCT WILL MORE THAN LIKELY NOT DO SHIT!" Actually, something that is worth trying is dropping three Alka-Seltzer tablets down the drain, then pouring in a cup of white vinegar. Wait several minutes, and then run the hot water for a while. If it works, you're like the Martha-freaking-Stewart of do-it-yourself plumbers.

If the Alka-Seltzer doesn't work on the drain, take a few

yourself and then slip on a sturdy pair of rubber gloves, grab a big-ass monkey wrench, and get in there and fix that sucker. You might also want to consider investing in a pair of knee pads. Sure, you'll look like a dork, but at least you'll be able to walk when you're done.

What You'll Need

> Monkey wrench (minimum two-inch jaw opening)
> Pipe brush or wire brush
> Small plastic bucket
> Knee pads (optional)
> Bio-Clean drain cleaner

How It's Done

The clog is most likely situated in one of two places: either all gunked up in a stanky, greasy blob around the stopper, or sitting pretty down in the drain trap (where the drain pipe curves back up before entering the wall).

Before you even get started, reach under the sink and turn both shutoff valves clockwise to turn off the water. Then place a bucket directly under the drain to catch any of the hell water that might leak out during this process.

Regardless of how you're going to try to unclog the drain, your first step will be to remove the stopper in the sink. If you're lucky, the stopper will just lift right out, or you can try turning it clockwise until it releases. More likely, though, you'll have to release the stopper by removing the pivot rod that's used to open and close the drain. If you look under the sink, you'll see the pivot rod coming out of the back of the drain pipe, and connecting to a strip of metal (known as a "clevis"—named, one can only assume, after its slack-jawed inventor) leading up to the faucet. The other end goes through a hole in the stopper, keep-

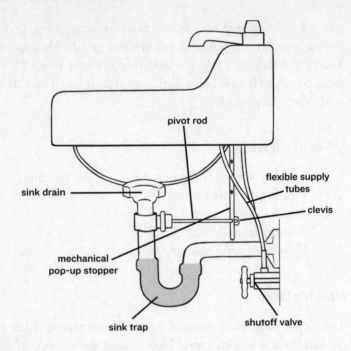

ing it in place. Unscrew the nut that holds the pivot rod to the drain pipe, either by hand or with a wrench. Then pull out the pivot rod and you'll be able to lift out the stopper. If the clog is up top near the stopper, the stem under the stopper will look like it has impaled itself on a small rodent that's been poached in motor oil, and will smell even worse. When you look down the drain, you'll just see a gunky black mess. Remember, use another sink or the tub to clean off the stopper and/or eventual vomit.

If the clog is at the top, you'll want to clean out the first section of drain pipe beneath the sink. To do this, use your monkey wrench to loosen the first slip nut (it'll probably connect a vertical metal pipe down into the drain trap). When that's done, pull down gently on the plastic pipe below to free the vertical pipe. Next, use a wire pipe cleaner (like a tiny version of the classic chimney sweep's tool) and plenty of hot water to flush the clog out of the pipe. Keep an eye on the bucket underneath to make sure it doesn't overflow. When you're done, reconnect the drain trap and tighten that slip nut.

If you can't see the clog, try using a plunger. Leaving the stopper out, screw the pivot rod back in. If your sink has an overflow hole, stuff a wet rag in there good and tight. Place a plunger flat over the drain hole and cover it with water. Now, start a-plungin'. Give it several sharp thrusts and then take the plunger away and see if the drain flows smoothly.

The last place to check is the drain trap. Before you remove the trap, make sure the bucket is underneath to collect the particularly nasty water that will run out. Next, loosen the slip nuts on either end of the trap, remove the trap, and clean it out. If it's been a while since the trap was last checked, you may see that some kind of viscous black goo has formed around the inside of the pipe. Just hold your nose and get at it with a wire brush. Reinstall the trap and check the drainage again.

If that still doesn't do it, it's probably time to call a plumber. If you're feeling particularly adventurous, it is possible that the clog is just a bit farther down the drain and can be reached by one of those small "hand snakes" that you can buy at your local hardware store. Just remove the trap again, and twist the snake line down through the pipe as far as it will go.

Regardless of whether you've fixed the clog yourself or hired a pro, you'll want to prevent future clogs. The best preventative maintenance for your drains is frequent flushing with plenty of hot water, and occasional applications of a professional drain cleaner like Bio-Clean, which eats away at buildup before it becomes a clog. You won't find Bio-Clean at basic hardware stores, so it's a great excuse to visit the magical wonderland of your local plumbing supply store.

IN THE KITCHEN

How to Become a Martini Guy

"I'm not talking a cup of cheap gin splashed over an ice cube. I'm talking satin, fire, and ice; Fred Astaire in a glass; surgical cleanliness; insight and comfort; redemption and absolution. I'm talking a martini."

—ANONYMOUS

There's something supremely masculine yet elegant about a martini, and everything about the drink reinforces that reputation. From Frank Sinatra to Ernest Hemingway to James Bond, the list of martini aficionados reads like a who's who of men's men. Becoming a martini guy requires simply learning a thing or two about the drink and then enjoying them frequently with a smooth, caressing indulgence. You'll find that everything you do and say takes on an incomparable charm and wit with a chilled martini in your hand.

If you don't already own martini glasses and a cocktail shaker, go out and buy them right now. While you're out, pick up a few different kinds of gin, a bottle of dry vermouth, cocktail olives, and toothpicks. When you get home, put the glasses, shaker, and gin in the freezer, and put the vermouth in the fridge.

Before we start mixing, a little background. A martini is a drink of gin and vermouth of ambiguous origin, garnished with olives or a twist of lemon. If you prefer vodka, by all means use vodka, but you've got a different drink, a vodka martini. Interestingly, James Bond's martini, the Vesper, calls for both gin *and* vodka.

To make a martini, put a few cubes of ice into the shaker. Add a few ounces of gin and a splash of vermouth—the proportions are totally up to you. The less vermouth, the drier the martini. Legend has it that Winston Churchill would pour the gin, look across the room at the vermouth bottle, then drink the gin. I prefer a proportion of about five to one.

To mix and chill your martini, you can either shake it vigorously or stir it. The distinction has less to do with the outcome than with the popular appeal of Ian Fleming's famous protagonist. As with so many of life's finer indulgences, it's really just a matter of taste. Shaking tends to strengthen the flavor a bit, but with a martini that's not necessarily a good thing. Shaking also adds a little air and bits of ice, which cloud the drink, while purists may demand their martini be crystal clear. Some may say that shaking "bruises" the gin, but that's not the case (a Bloody Mary can be bruised—meaning the tomato juice breaks down and becomes watery—but that's not an issue with a martini). I would say, do whatever you like. There may be one real benefit to shaking your martini: A 1999 article in the *British Medical Journal* found that shaken martinis had significantly better antioxidant properties than stirred martinis. No wonder 007 seemed to have nine lives.

Strain the drink into a chilled martini glass, and garnish with either olives or a twist of lemon peel. When garnishing your martini with olives, always use an odd number (either one or three, or possibly five if your wife tends to nosh while you're drinking). The odd number is borrowed from the old Sicilian tradition of only serving an odd number of coffee beans in a glass of sambuca. Legend has it that an odd number of beans welcomes your guests, while an even number was a sign that you might soon meet with rather unfortunate circumstances (Fredo Corleone may have found two beans in his sambuca just before Al Neri took him out fishing).

To make a lemon twist, cut a thin sliver of lemon rind with a sharp knife. Rub the rind around the rim of the glass, give it a good, firm twist to release the oils, and drop it into the glass.

Variations

The classic martini, as described above, is served "neat," straight up in a martini glass. Martinis can also be served "on the rocks," with ice in a tumbler. There are innumerable variations on the recipe, but the only one true purists will accept is the "dirty martini," which calls for the addition of a splash of brine from the olive jar.

Martini Moments

Martinis are best when they're ice cold. That means you should always hold your glass by the stem, so your hands don't warm the drink.

A black tie ensemble is not required for martini drinking, although nothing accessorizes a tux quite like a cool martini. Martinis add a bit of maturity and class to any get-together (see "How to Win Over Her Parents," page 42). Be sure to keep all your supplies chilled and at the ready, since you'll never know when you might be called upon to make your famous martinis.

How to Make a Cosmopolitan

If you learn how to make only one drink in your entire life (of course, you already know how to make martinis), make that drink a cosmopolitan. For one simple reason: It's the single greatest chick drink ever. More kick than a wine cooler, more class than a strawberry daiquiri. If you can make a killer cosmo, you'll score major points with her girlfriends, her mother, and just about anyone else who sidles up to the bar. Let's face it, everyone loves the bartender, and they'll love you that much more when you're mixing up delicious batches of that potent pink elixir.

There's no clear origin to the drink, although most roads lead to the thriving gay community in Provincetown, Massachusetts. It makes sense, since Provincetown sits out there at the tip of Cape Cod and occupies its own unique reality, that they'd take the classic Cape Codder (vodka and cranberry juice) and give it a head-to-toe makeover befitting the guys on *Queer Eye for the Straight Guy*. The result is a drink with irrepressible style and plenty of great taste. And, don't forget, it still packs quite a punch.

Here's how it's made:

1½ ounces vodka—try citrus-infused vodka like Grey Goose
    L'Orange or Absolut Citron

1 ounce Cointreau or triple sec

I ounce cranberry juice
Splash of fresh lime juice

Put a few ice cubes in a cocktail shaker. Add the vodka, Cointreau, and juices. Shake until well chilled and strain into a chilled martini glass.

You can garnish your cosmo with a maraschino cherry or a twist of lime or orange. To make a twist, slice a thin sliver of lime or orange rind. Twist it tightly over the drink to release the oils, and then drop it in.

As with the garnish, the ingredients and proportions are completely up to you. Try different kinds of vodkas, or add a little more cranberry juice or a little less lime juice. You can't go wrong with a cosmo (FYI, always use fresh lime juice, never Rose's or other bottled juice), so master your own particular recipe and just be sure to always have the ingredients on hand.

How to Set the Table

Most men can't even fathom the concept of a napkin, let alone come to terms with the whole formal place-setting enigma. But with just a little bit of concentration, and an eye for detail, any guy can master the art of setting the table. This information is not only useful for fine dining at home, but from now on, whenever you're eating in a formal setting you'll be able to reach for the proper water glass with comfort, and know that you don't have to lick your salad fork clean and save it for later.

First of all, you need to realize that there is a logical system at play here. Cutlery is set out on the side where most people are likely to be comfortable using it. So knives and soup spoons go on the right, since most people are right-handed. Forks go on the left for the same reason. If you want to totally blow your guests away, reverse the setting for a left-handed guest, and seat them at a left corner so they'll have plenty of elbow room. If your mother-in-law is left-handed, this is a perfect opportunity to win her over. Also, the order of placement is meant to coincide with the order in which each utensil will be used. The outermost utensil will be used first, and you'll move inward toward the plate with each subsequent course. Here's how it all comes together:

If you're using placemats, center each one directly in front of each chair, about one inch away from the edge of the table.

Place the main service plate in the middle of the placemat.

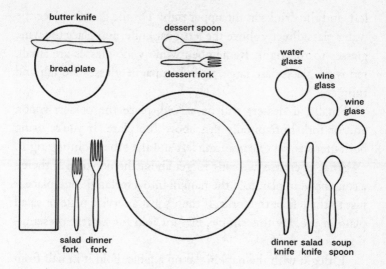

If soup and/or salad will be served, that bowl or plate should be set on top of the service plate.

As mentioned above, utensils are placed next to the plate, in order from the outside in, with forks on the left and knives and spoons on the right. (If you ever forget, here's a tip my friend Steve Weiss used when teaching his kids how to set the table: The words "fork" and "left" both have four letters, while "knife," "spoon," and "right" have five.) Knives are placed with the cutting edge facing in toward the plate. This is a custom dating back to ancient times, meant to express goodwill toward your guests. Once you know what's being served, you'll know exactly which utensils you'll need and where they go.

Here's another great tip from domestic god Steve Weiss to help you remember which side is for bread, and which is for drinks. Hold your hands out in front of you, and bring each thumb and index finger together, holding your middle finger straight up. You'll see you've formed a *b* with your left hand and a *d* with your right. So the bread plate and knife go in the upper left, and the drinks in the upper right. For the glasses, place the water glass directly above the leftmost knife, and place the wine glasses to the right. Remember, white wine glasses are small, red wine glasses are large, and champagne glasses are tall and thin.

Finally, if dessert will be served, place the dessert spoon and/or fork horizontally just above the plate. If you're using both utensils, set one pointing left and the other pointing right.

And, of course, we can't forget about the napkins. If there's a soup bowl in play, fold the napkin into a rectangle and place it just to the left of the forks. If there's just a service plate or salad plate in use, try this simple, elegant fold for a great presentation:

1. Begin with the napkin flat on a table. Fold it in half from corner to corner, to form a triangle. Turn it so the long side is closest to you.

2. Grasp each of the two bottom corners, and fold them up to the top, forming a diamond, with a small channel running down the middle.

3. Now grab each of the side corners and lift so the napkin folds into a triangle again.

4. Finally, fold the napkin away from you so the two corners meet, then stand the napkin upright on a plate, with the two "wings" in the back slightly apart for stability.

So there it is, one of the great mysteries of the ages laid bare before you. Unfortunately, with great knowledge comes great responsibility. By that I mean now that you know how it's done, your wife will expect you to do it right from now on. Come to think of it, that's true for just about everything in this book. Sorry about that. Hopefully it'll help you get some after all the dinner guests leave.

How to Look Like a Chef

My brother's college roommate used to cook up a little garlic in olive oil whenever he'd invite a girl over for dinner. The place smelled so good when she got there, it didn't matter what dinner actually tasted like. The point is, there are many things you can do, short of actually cooking palatable food, to create the impression that you're not a total buffoon in the kitchen. Here are a few simple techniques you can try to make it look like you know what you're doing.

First, let's deal with the outfit. Forget about buying chef's whites or that ridiculous chimney hat (it's actually called a "toque"). You don't even need an apron, unless you're planning on whipping up some biscuits in a tuxedo. All you really need is a clean kitchen towel tucked into your belt or waistband, and a cocktail within arm's reach at all times. That way, you'll exude an air of relaxed confidence, or you can just keep drinking until you do.

Next, let's talk about the kitchen setup. You've seen all those cooking shows where the countertop is perfectly arranged with all the ingredients premeasured or chopped. This technique is called *mise en place* (pronounced "meez on plahs"), a French term meaning "to put in place." It simply means that you do all the hard work ahead of time, and when you're actually cooking it's just a matter of throwing the ingredients in. It makes everything look so easy, and makes you look like a master chef. So read through your recipes and gather everything together. One strategy is to place all your herbs, spices, and garlic together on a saucer, and place larger chopped items in little bowls. Make sure perishable ingredients make their way back to the fridge after you've prepped them.

Nothing raises doubts about your culinary prowess like a desperate plea for Band-Aids or a tourniquet emanating from behind the kitchen door. To avoid cutting yourself, it is essential to keep your knives very sharp (when your knives get dull, use one of those tabletop sharpeners where you slide the blade through a groove) and learn a simple chopping technique. Sharp knives allow you to cut through meats and vegetables easily, without slipping. When you're chopping something, hold it down with your fingers tucked under so your nails are flat against the food and your knuckles are facing the knife. Chop with the blade leaning up against your knuckles at a slight angle, and just slide your hand back along the food as you cut. That way, there's no chance of getting your fingers caught under the blade. You'll also find that with practice this can be a very fast way to get your chopping done. You'll be chopping like Jacques Pépin in no time.

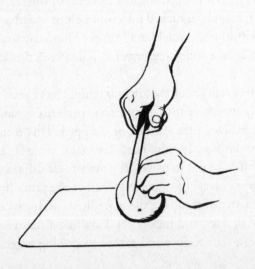

A couple of other techniques to sell your skills involve seasoning and testing. When you're getting all your ingredients together, pour a few tablespoons of salt (use kosher or sea salt for added effect) and pepper in two small bowls. As you're cooking, season along the way with pinches of salt and pepper from the bowls. You may sprinkle the spices from a foot or two above the pan for even distribution. Under no circumstance should your seasoning be accompanied by wild gesticulations or any monosyllabic barkings even remotely similar to "Bam." That would just be silly.

Testing your food along the way is crucial to getting it right. Don't be shy. Use your fingers to poke at things to make sure they're done, and get a little lick of sauce to see if it needs salt or pepper. After all, that's why you've got a kitchen towel on your hip.

Finally, here are three techniques that look so cool, they should be in any chef wannabe's repertoire.

Using a Sharpening Steel

You may have seen a real chef grab a knife and then with a quick flick of the wrist run the blade along a metal rod. It's a very *Iron Chef* move. That rod is called a "sharpening steel." Oddly enough, sharpening steels aren't used for sharpening, but for honing. Honing doesn't sharpen a dull knife, it only fine-tunes a sharp knife to keep it straight and true. So while you only need to sharpen your knives when they get dull, you should hone them on a sharpening steel before each use.

First and foremost, and I can't stress this enough, start slowly when you're learning how to use a steel. It takes a lot of practice to get comfortable with it, so take your time. Hold the steel in your off hand, with the guard protecting your thumb and fingers. Start with the handle end of the knife blade high up on the steel. Press the edge of the blade against the steel at about a twenty-five-degree angle, and draw the blade across and down the steel until you reach the tip of the knife blade. Repeat five times. Then bring the knife blade back up along the other side of the steel, press the opposite edge of the blade against the steel and pull it down and across again, and repeat on that side five times. Then repeat the honing three times on each side, then two times, and then one last time on each side. You should now have a perfectly honed knife, and be well on your way to earning "the people's ovation and fame forever." *Arigato*, Chairman Kaga.

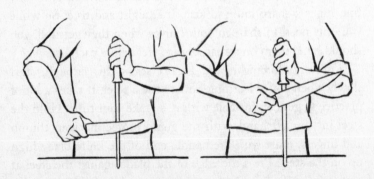

The Skillet Flip

If you've ever watched a cooking show, you've probably seen this trick. The chef will be cooking up vegetables or shrimp, and he'll just flick the pan and the food will flip up and over itself. A few more flips, and everything in the pan will be evenly cooked. It's a very useful technique, and it looks super-cool. It's quite easy, although it takes a little practice.

To learn the skillet flip, put about a cup of dry beans in a cold skillet (make sure it has a curved or slanted side, not straight). Hold the pan out in front of you, and give it a quick shake to make sure everything's loose. Quickly and firmly, push the pan away from you about four to six inches and then pull it back a couple of inches. The beans should slide forward, and then the leading edge of beans should climb the far edge up and out of the pan. To complete the motion, push the pan back out a few inches, and the flipped contents should land back toward the middle of the pan. As you're starting out, try tilting the pan down a bit away from you; that should make the flip a bit easier to execute.

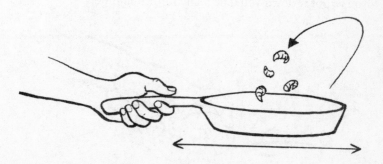

The One-Handed Egg Break

Breaking an egg with one hand isn't nearly as useful as the skillet flip, but it's so cool I just had to include it. I learned this technique from my father-in-law, Martin Bendersky, who has mastered this and many other kitchen arts. In fact, he's one of the finest gourmet chefs I know, as well as a brilliant scholar and a snappy dresser (see "How to Win Over Her Parents," page 42).

To get started, place the egg on the counter in front of you so that the longer axis of the egg is perpendicular to you. Grab the egg gently with your cracking hand between your thumb, index, and middle fingers. Your thumb should be at the center (on the "equator," if you will), with the top half of the egg firmly tucked in the crook of your index finger and the bottom half cradled by your middle finger. Crack the egg on the point right between your two fingertips. Pull back gently with your fingers, and use your thumb to gently pull the bottom half of the shell away from the top. Raise the egg up for dramatic effect and let the yolk and the white drop into the bowl. The one-handed break takes a lot of practice to perfect, but once you've got it down you'll be ready for prime time.

How to Purchase, Prepare, and Serve Seafood

Difficulty
T T T
Reward
♥ ♥ ♥ ♥

Imagine the scenario: a breezy summer evening on Cape Cod, the Jersey shore, or wherever. A bunch of old friends are getting together for a perfect seaside dinner. Someone has to step up and prepare the meal that will bring this beer-commercial moment to life. The perfect husband must have, in his bag of tricks, a few essential techniques for buying and preparing seafood. This is a basic introduction to some of the most popular seafood. There's an incredible variety available, so once you've mastered these, expand your horizons and try everything else.

Purchasing

Unless you've got a high-end supermarket nearby, one you can definitely trust, always seek out a reputable fish market for your purchases. You'll know the place, it'll be the one with the parking lot full every afternoon during the summer, towering stacks of empty bushel baskets out back, and a no-nonsense staff that answers your questions and will always go in the back to find the perfect fillet for you.

Let's start off with the basics: salmon and tuna. Once you've gotten comfortable with these, then you can branch out. For whole salmon, check the eyes and gills. The eyes should be clear, not cloudy, and the gills should be bright, deep red. The fish should have a bright sheen to it. Ask the fishmonger to fillet it for you. Fillets of salmon or tuna steaks should be bright in color, without any noticeable oily film. The flesh should hold together firmly, and have only a slight aroma. Also keep in mind that while whole fish can be kept on ice, fillets shouldn't be, since the water from the melting ice will hasten the deterioration of the fish. If the market is displaying fillets directly on ice, you may want to think about looking elsewhere. If fish is the main course, plan on about half a pound per person. Remember, put all seafood in the refrigerator as soon as you get home.

Make sure shrimp and scallops are firm and don't smell too fishy. For boiled or sauteed shrimp, purchase large or extra large, but avoid the jumbos. For sea scallops, look for the largest they've got, although make sure they still hold together nicely at that size. Three to four shrimp per person makes a great appetizer, and three or four large sea scallops is plenty for a main course.

If oysters and clams are on the menu, they absolutely must be alive when purchased. The live ones will have their shells tightly clamped shut. Open clams and oysters may also still be alive. Just squeeze them closed a few times, and they should lock shut. If they don't, they're dead and should be thrown away. If there are several varieties of oysters available, ask the vendor which he would recommend. Oyster and clam eaters will easily go through a half dozen per person, but check ahead to find out who will actually eat them.

Lobsters should be alive and kicking. When they're taken from the tank, look for the telltale flap of the tail to know they're feisty. Don't accept lobsters that just hang down in the claws and tail. If lobster is your main course, a one-and-a-quarter- to one-and-a-half-pounder per person should be plenty.

Other supplies: butter, lemons, shrimp deveiner, claw crackers, oyster/clam knife, steamer pot, bug spray, corn, beer, and more beer.

Preparing

For fish, keep it simple. Salmon and tuna work great marinated in Soy Vay or other fine Asian marinades and then grilled. By the way, those fish-grilling baskets work really well and keep your fish from sticking. With salmon, you want to grill them for about four to six minutes per half inch of thickness, turning halfway through. When the fish feels about the same consistency as your flexed forearm, it's done. With tuna, you really want to sear it quickly, just a few minutes on each side, and leave it basically raw in the middle.

Shrimp should be peeled and "deveined." To do this, place the shrimp on its side on a cutting board. Insert the deveiner or a small knife (serrated steak knives work pretty well) into the small hole on the thick end, and work it toward the tail, cutting through the top of the shell. Peel off the shell and wash out the "vein" (actually it's the digestive tract) running down the back. Drop the shrimp into a bowl of heavily salted water to firm them up (this is called "brining"). Rinse them thoroughly before cooking, then either boil or sauté them very quickly, until they turn bright pink and firm. For boiled shrimp, plunge them into ice water as soon as they're cooked.

Scallops should be rinsed, seasoned with salt and pepper on both sides, and then pan fried in a little olive oil until browned on each side, about six to eight minutes. Test for doneness by poking the scallops with a finger. They're done when they reach the consistency of a flexed forearm.

Oysters and clams should be scrubbed clean and kept in the refrigerator until just before they're prepared. Clams can be steamed, which just involves setting up a steamer pot and steaming the clams until they open up (about ten to fifteen minutes). Discard any unopened clams, since they were probably dead before cooking. Reserve the cooking broth for later.

Oysters are best raw (also called "on the half shell"). To serve these, you've got to learn the art of shucking. To open up these little suckers, you'll need a shucking knife, a tough, steel mesh glove, and a thick towel. Lay an oyster flat in the towel in your gloved hand, with the more rounded side down on your palm (that'll keep more of the delicious, briny liquor with the oyster). With the joint of the shell facing inward, pry into the little gap with the knife and twist until you hear a small pop. Remove the top shell and run the knife underneath the oyster to separate it completely. Keep the shucked oysters on a bed of ice until ready to serve.

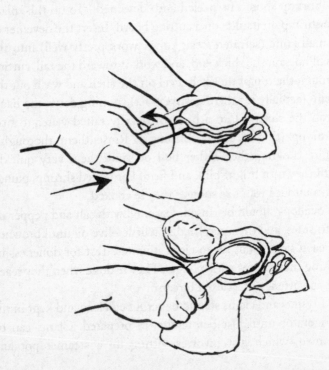

The easiest way to cook lobsters is simply to boil them. In a large stock pot, bring about two and a half quarts of salted water per lobster to a boil. Add the lobsters, putting them into the water headfirst, being careful not to overfill the pot. Bring the water back to a boil and cook for about twelve to fifteen minutes. When they're done, drain the lobsters, let them cool a bit, and serve. One trick for draining the water from cooked lobsters is to cut off the tips of their claws with kitchen shears or a cleaver, then drain them in a colander with the claws toward the bottom.

Serving

If you're hosting a big seafood dinner, cleanup can be a nightmare. To make it easy, put down a layer of trash bags or plastic sheeting over the table, then cover that with two or three layers of newspaper. After dinner, simply roll everything up and throw it away. Just make sure your trash cans have tight-fitting lids, otherwise you'll wake to find that seagulls, raccoons, and any number of nocturnal critters have turned your driveway into an all-night buffet.

Really fresh fish should be served as simply as possible. You won't need tartar sauce or other condiments to cover up the flavor.

Boiled shrimp are great with cocktail sauce. If you don't have bottled sauce, you can make your own by mixing ketchup and horseradish. This is the best way to go if you like spicy foods, since you can make the sauce as hot as you like.

Scallops have such a great sweet and briny flavor, you don't need to add anything to them.

Serve up steamed clams with the clam broth and drawn butter. Don't even think of skimming those delicious milk fats off the top of the butter—that's where all the great flavor comes from.

Oysters should be served on a plate of crushed ice. If you're an oyster novice, recognize that these slimy little guys are not really meant to be chewed, just swallowed whole (though if the oysters are very large, rest assured that chewing is, of course, preferable to asphyxiation). You can add a dab of cocktail sauce to each one, then just pick them up, shell and all, hold the edge to your mouth, and slide them down. Another option is to make oyster shooters: Drop an oyster into a shot glass, then top with a dash of Tabasco sauce and a splash of vodka.

Serve up a whole lobster per person, with plenty of melted butter for dipping. To eat the lobster, break off the claws and crack them with a mallet just below the joint of the claw itself. You can also get at the knuckle meat with a mallet. Break off all the legs and line them up next to one another. With a beer bottle or rolling pin, roll over the legs firmly from the thin ends to

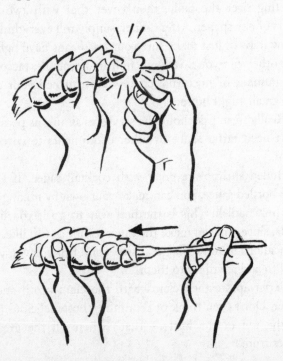

the thick. Little rods of meat should be forced out the end. Break off the tail where it meets the body. Then snap off all the flat flippers at the very end. Use your thumb to push up into the tail and force all the tail meat out the other end.

Now, inside the body you've got this green glop, known as "tomalley," which is the only nonmandatory part of the lobster. It's actually the internal organs of the lobster. It is edible, and some people consider it a delicacy, but I'll leave that for you to decide.

And, did I mention, make sure there's plenty of beer.

How to Carve a Turkey

Standing above a perfectly roasted turkey, carving knife in hand, cranberry sauce and gravy poised like two six-shooters strapped to your hips, you strike the most enduring Norman Rockwell pose this modern world will allow. Long after women have achieved complete equality and most likely far surpassed men in everything except, possibly, the volume of bodily excretions produced daily, turkey carving will remain firmly the divine province of man. And since you don't get too many practice birds, here are some simple instructions to do it right the first time and every time.

If you're a novice carver, do not bring that bird anywhere near the dining room table. To hell with Rockwell, this is the last vestige of your masculine pride we're talking about. Until you're completely comfortable with carving, you should always do the deed in the privacy of the kitchen (preferably one with a door that locks). Keep in mind that your guests will still be able to hear your foul, frustrated ranting, and also that the dull, greasy thud of a perfectly roasted turkey hitting the kitchen floor is clearly discernible from the dining room.

1. When the turkey comes out of the oven, let it rest for at least fifteen minutes. This allows the juices to redistribute throughout the bird, keeping the meat moist and making carving easier. Take this time to sharpen a large carving knife (see "How to Look Like a Chef," page 157) and mix yourself a stiff drink (see "How to Become a Martini Guy," page 149). You

want a very sharp knife to make clean cuts through the meat, which will help keep it juicy.

2. Transfer the turkey from the roasting pan to a large cutting board. If you're right-handed, have the legs to the right (reverse if you're left-handed). We'll work on one side of the bird at a time. At all times you can hold the bird steady with a large fork or just use your hand. Pull the leg and thigh away from the body, and cut through the skin down to the bone. Press the leg and thigh down onto the board and gently pull back. If that doesn't separate the thigh joint, just probe with the point of your knife until you find the joint and cut through it.

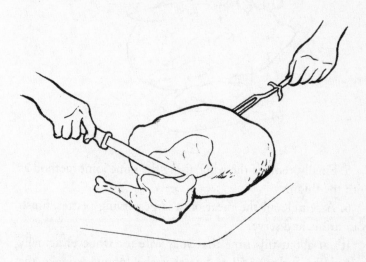

3. Use the same technique to separate the leg from the thigh. You can either serve these parts whole or carve them up. To carve the leg: Hold it upside-down by the bone, with the meaty part on the cutting board. Cut parallel to the bone to remove slices of meat. To carve the thigh: Place it skin-side down. Cut along both sides of the bone, and then cut underneath the ends to release the bone. Then cut the thigh into slices.

4. Leaving the wings on the body for stability, cut horizontally just above the wing, along the bottom edge of the breast. Then cut vertical slices off the breast down to this point. You could also use the French technique of cutting off the entire breast, slicing it, and presenting the whole thing together.

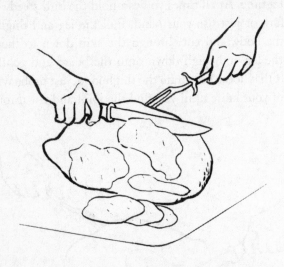

5. Finally, remove the wing, using the same joint method as with the thigh.

6. Assemble all the meat on a large serving platter, finish your drink, and serve.

It's at about this time that your wife (or whoever actually cooked the turkey) will realize that she forgot to make the gravy. If you want to enter the Perfect Husband pantheon, here's a great last-minute gravy recipe:

1. Pour all the drippings from the roasting pan into a measuring cup or any heatproof container large enough to hold it all. The fat will rise to the top.

2. Squeeze the bulb of a turkey baster, and then plunge the other end down through the fat to the bottom. Release the bulb to draw the thick broth into the baster. Squeeze it out into

another cup. Continue until you've transferred all of the broth, and discard the fat.

3. In a small cup, mix about one tablespoon of cornstarch in two tablespoons of water. Use your finger to mix it up good.

4. Now place the roasting pan over two burners on the stove, both on high. Pour a good splash of white wine or sherry into the pan, and scrape up all the turkey bits stuck to the bottom. When the pan is pretty much clean, pour the scrapings and wine into a saucepan over medium heat.

5. Add the other drippings, and then stir in the cornstarch mixture to thicken the gravy. If it gets too thick you can stir in a little more wine or water. Add salt and pepper to taste, pour it into a gravy boat, and serve.

How to Make a Stir-Fry

Difficulty

𝑇 𝑇 𝑇

Reward

♥ ♥ ♥

If you learn to make only one dish, there's nothing easier, more versatile, and healthier than a good stir-fry. You can include just about any vegetables and meats, and the whole thing comes together really quickly in a single pan. Of course, there are a few things you'll need to know before getting started, but once we get these out of the way, you'll be whipping up excellent stir-fries before you can say "Kung POW!"

There are countless recipes for stir-frying, but I've chosen to defer to the brilliant minds over at *Cook's Illustrated*, the home of America's Test Kitchen. These guys try every recipe several different ways, then compare and contrast the outcomes to figure out the best one. They've studied stir-frying extensively, and their technique works great every time. By the way, if you want to look like a chef, get a subscription to *Cook's Illustrated* magazine, read every issue, and display them prominently in your kitchen.

First of all, don't worry if you don't have a wok. It turns out the standard stove burner isn't powerful enough to heat the tall, curved surface of the wok completely. You're better off with a large frying pan, preferably nonstick.

Next, choose your ingredients. Pretty much anything will work, like broccoli, mushrooms, peppers, eggplant, spinach, and carrots on the vegetable side, and chicken, beef, pork, or shrimp on the meat side. And if you think it's the kind of thing your wife would appreciate, you should seriously consider tofu as a meat substitute. Pick a few different vegetables and one meat. If you're using shrimp, see "How to Purchase, Prepare, and Serve Seafood" (page 163) for preparation suggestions.

Preparation is really the key to keeping the stir-fry fast and easy. You want to get everything chopped and prepared ahead of time, so you can just throw them into the hot pan, give a few quick stirs, and you're done. So, let's use the *mise en place* technique, as discussed in "How to Look Like a Chef" (page 157). Chop the vegetables and meat into nice, bite-sized pieces, collect them in small bowls or plates (you should cut meat on a separate board with a different knife, and always wash your hands immediately afterward to avoid any possible salmonella contamination).

For the vegetables, group them together in the order they'll go in the pan, from the longest cooking to the shortest. The longest cooking veggies (Group I) are peppers, onions, and carrots. Then you'll want to add broccoli and green beans (Group II). Next is celery, mushrooms, and zucchini (Group III), and finally scallions, tomatoes, spinach, and any other greens or herbs (Group IV).

Regardless of which meat you're using, you'll want to marinate it for at least an hour or so, for extra flavor. It's really simple: Just cut the meat into bite-sized slices (thin slices for beef, pork, or chicken, one-inch cubes for shrimp or tofu), place them into a Ziploc bag, then pour in equal parts soy sauce and dry sherry. To keep all the meat covered with marinade, force all the air out of the bag, to the point where the marinade is just about to spill out the top. Then seal the bag, and you'll see that all the meat stays covered.

Any good stir-fry should have chopped garlic and fresh ginger. Here are some quick techniques for preparing these "aromatics":

Garlic: Chop the flat, root end off each clove. With the heel of your palm, give a solid smack to each clove. This should loosen the husk and make it easy to peel off. Then lay a large chopping knife flat over the clove, with the blade facing away from you. Using the heel of your palm again, smash the clove under the blade. With a quick couple of chops you'll have perfectly minced garlic.

Ginger: The hardest part about preparing ginger root is figuring out how to peel it. The best way is to use the edge of a spoon, and just roughly scrape it clean. Then cut off about an inch of the root and chop it as fine as possible (see the chopping technique in "How to Look Like a Chef," page 157).

Finally, you'll need a sauce for your stir-fry. To keep things simple, I'd recommend buying one of those small packets of stir-fry sauce mix in the Asian foods section of the supermarket. Follow the simple instructions on the package and set the sauce aside until you're ready to add it. In a pinch, just combine some soy sauce, sherry, and a little sesame oil.

Now that you've got everything prepared, let's get a-cookin'! This recipe creates about four servings. You can either halve the recipe if it's just the two of you, or make the whole thing and enjoy leftovers.

3–4 tablespoons oil (peanut or canola are best)

¾–1 pound meat, shrimp, or tofu

Equal parts (about 1 tablespoon) soy sauce and dry sherry

1–1½ pounds vegetables

1 tablespoon chopped garlic, or more to taste

1 tablespoon chopped fresh ginger, or more to taste

Handful of unsalted peanuts or cashews (optional)

Stir-fry sauce mix (see above)

1 tablespoon cornstarch

1. Place a large frying pan over high heat for a few minutes, until you can feel the heat coming off it. Add about 1 tablespoon of oil and heat until it just starts to smoke.

2. Drain the meat as much as possible, and add to the hot oil (you may want to keep a large lid handy to keep the initial oil spatter to a minimum). Stir-fry the meat until it's not quite cooked completely, about 20 seconds for shrimp, 1 minute for beef or pork, or 3 minutes for chicken. (For tofu, try to brown the pieces on all sides.) Use a slotted spoon to transfer the meat to a bowl.

3. Keeping the pan very hot, add another tablespoon of oil. Add the vegetables in the order mentioned on page 175. Cook each group for about 2 to 3 minutes before adding the next group, then add the last group and stir-fry for about 30 seconds.

4. Clear out a little space in the middle of the pan and add the ginger and garlic with a little additional oil. Stir them up quickly and firmly, then turn off the heat and mix everything together.

5. Crank up the heat again, and return the meat to the pan. Add the nuts, if you want. Then give a quick stir to the sauce and pour it over, stirring to coat everything. To thicken the sauce, combine the cornstarch with 2 tablespoons water and stir it into the sauce. Serve immediately over white rice, and be sure to use a serving spoon to drizzle the sauce over the top.

Once you get the basics down, you can improvise in all kinds of cool ways. Try different combinations of vegetables and meats, or add a kick with a bit of chili paste, which you can find in many supermarkets these days (or any Asian market).

Note: Subscriptions to *Cook's Illustrated,* cooking tips, product reviews, and much more can be obtained on their website at www.cooksillustrated.com.

How to Make Tiramisu

Difficulty
T T

Reward
♥ ♥ ♥ ♥

You get instant kitchen cred with tiramisu. It's trendy, exotic, and amazingly easy (I've got a friend whose kitchen repertoire consists exclusively of Minute Rice and tiramisu). Plus it's got chocolate, coffee, and booze, which is always a great combination. Legend has it that tiramisu (which translates literally as "pick me up" in Italian) was originally a favorite of Venetian courtesans who needed an extra jolt of energy for a busy night's work. So it's got that going for it, too. Finally, tiramisu is one of those forgiving recipes that you can screw up completely until the final step. Then you cover it all up and nobody's the wiser.

These days, all of the ingredients can be found in most supermarkets. If not, try to find an Italian specialty store, which is great for all kinds of delicious goodies.

½ cup sugar, plus more for coffee
6 egg yolks
Pinch of salt
1 pound mascarpone cheese
3 cups strong coffee
½ cup Kahlua or other coffee liqueur
36 ladyfingers
¼ cup cocoa powder

1. In a medium-size bowl, combine the sugar, egg yolks (see Technical Tip below), salt, and cheese. Whisk vigorously until creamy and slightly pale. Put bowl in the refrigerator.

2. Brew the coffee (or use instant coffee to make it easy), add sugar to taste, and combine with Kahlua in a small bowl.

3. Find a nice, medium-size glass or ceramic serving bowl for the tiramisu.

4. Dip a ladyfinger into the coffee, then remove it, let it drain quickly and place it in the bottom of the serving bowl. Repeat to make a complete layer of ladyfingers.

5. Pour and spread just enough of the cheese mixture over the ladyfingers to cover.

6. Sprinkle a generous layer of cocoa over the cheese.

7. Add additional layers to fill the bowl. You can either sprinkle just a little cocoa on the top layer, or cover it completely to hide any imperfections. Refrigerate for at least an hour before serving, or even longer for richer flavor. Makes about 6 servings, with leftovers.

Technical Tip

An easy way to separate eggs is to gently break the egg into a small bowl, keeping the yolk intact, and then just reach in and grab the yolk, draining the whites between your fingers.

How to Make Crème Brûlée

There may be no more arousing question you could ask your wife than this: "Honey, where do we keep the ramekins?" Never heard of ramekins? They're small, shallow ceramic dishes, usually white (your sports bar may use ramekins if you ask for extra Cheez Whiz with your nachos). Never felt the urge to make crème brûlée? Well, you should. It's the grand dame of all desserts and earns you major points with the wife. It's incredibly easy to make and, most important, you get to fire up the butane torch you bought for soldering up those new plumbing lines (see "How to Solder a Pipe," page 113).

Let's get started making your first crème brûlée. Everything except for the final step should be done well before dinner. In terms of equipment, you'll need a saucepan, mixing bowls, a deep baking dish, an electric mixer, a whisk, four six-ounce ramekins, and, of course, the butane torch.

2 cups heavy cream
I teaspoon vanilla extract
6 egg yolks
½ cup sugar, plus 4 tablespoons

I. Preheat oven to 325 degrees. Pour the cream into a medium saucepan. Cook over low heat until hot. Don't let the cream boil. Turn off the heat and let the cream cool for a few minutes. Stir the vanilla extract into the cream.

2. Separate the egg yolks by carefully breaking the eggs into a small bowl, then reach in and gently lift out the yolks (let the whites drain off between your fingers). Combine the egg yolks and sugar in a mixing bowl and beat them together with an electric mixer until pale yellow in color.

3. Pour about one-quarter of the cream into the egg-sugar mixture and whisk together. Then pour all of this back into the cream and stir until blended.

4. Place four ramekins on a baking pan (not a shallow cookie sheet, but a metal or glass pan with walls about 2 inches high). Use a ladle to evenly divide the cream mixture between the ramekins. Boil several cups of water and pour it into the baking pan about halfway up the sides of the ramekins.

5. Bake for about 30 minutes, or until the edges are firm but the center is still jiggly. Remove the ramekins from the baking pan. Let them cool, and then place them in the refrigerator until thoroughly chilled.

6. When you're ready to serve, sprinkle one tablespoon of sugar atop each custard. Light the butane torch and quickly cook the sugar until it's slightly blackened (it should taste like a marshmallow burned over a campfire).

That's it, you're done. All that remains are the adoring accolades and possibly some post-brûlée nookie.

How to Do the Dishes (all of them!)

I know exactly the way most husbands operate. When it's your turn to do the dishes, you do just enough of a half-assed job so your wife will grab the sponge from your hand, expel you from the kitchen with a pat on the *tuchus,* and finish the job herself. That's actually not a bad short-term strategy, but I wouldn't rely on it for too long. Remember, wives are vengeful creatures, and she won't soon forget your trickery. Face it, one way or another, you're going to have to do the dishes. So why not make the process as painless as possible?

Before Cooking

As we learned in "How to Look Like a Chef" (page 157), using the French technique of *mise en place* goes a long way to convincing onlookers that you know what you're doing. But it also pays off big-time when cleanup comes around. Keeping everything organized, with many ingredients on little plates and bowls, helps prevent the mess from spreading in an ever-expanding blob, fouling every flat surface in the kitchen. When you prepare using *mise en place,* you can simply put things away as you use them, and stack the empty bowls and plates in the sink when you're done. It takes a little more work in the beginning, but it'll mean less to clean up in the end.

During Cooking

The best thing you can do to lessen the after-dinner cleanup is to clean as you go. If you're cooking, you'll notice there's plenty of downtime, when you're waiting for things to finish or cool a bit just before serving. So leave the dishwasher open while you're cooking, and use any downtime to do a quick cleanup of the kitchen. The food has yet to harden onto the plates and utensils, so just give a quick rinse and throw them in the dishwasher. Your goal here should be to have everything cleaned except the cups, plates, and utensils you're using for the actual meal.

Your Last Hope

If you have no other options, and you're facing a sink piled halfway to the ceiling with crusty pots and pans, there is still hope for you. Zen master, poet, and peace activist Thich Nhat Hanh wrote: "There are two ways to wash the dishes. The first is to wash the dishes in order to have clean dishes and the second is to wash the dishes in order to wash the dishes." The point is, if all you do is think about what else you could be doing while washing the dishes, it becomes a major chore that stands between you and a cold beer and the last innings of the ball game. Rather, you could embrace the moments you spend at the sink, focusing on your breathing and paying close attention to your actions. It can be a very pleasant feeling, using this simple technique to appreciate an otherwise laborious moment. So next time you're faced with doing the dishes, don't just do the dishes to get it over with, but do the dishes to do the dishes. Simple enough, eh?

The Unfinished Unload

Finally, there's this phenomenon where men will unload most of the dishes in the dishwasher, but not all, or will just leave the dishes in the drying rack forever (by the way, this is caused by the same part of the male brain that prevents us from putting our clothes away). The way to overcome this is to think of the kitchen cabinets the same way that you think of your toolbox or your tackle box: everything in its place, so nothing gets lost. Granted, misplacing the gravy boat isn't nearly as big a deal as losing a hex wrench or that new crystal butt hopper trout fly, but thinking of them the same way could help you just put all the damn dishes away at once, and thus become a more perfect husband.

ON THE TOWN

How to Wait Patiently Until She's Ready to Leave

Difficulty
𝐓 𝐓 𝐓 𝐓

Reward
♥ ♥

How many of you have asked yourself, "What could she possibly be doing up there for so long?" Here's a little exercise to put yourself in her shoes and understand why it's absolutely impossible for the two of you to get out the door on time. Next time you're getting ready to go out with the guys, put on a suit and tie. Then, about two minutes before you were planning on leaving, run upstairs, spin around twenty times fast, strip down to your undies, and then get dressed appropriately. Now you know what she goes through every time the two of you go out. And there's not a damn thing you can do about it. So rather than pacing anxiously, wringing your hands raw, and every so often slamming your head against a wall, let's explore some more productive tactics to help pass those interminable minutes before she's really ready to leave.

First of all, you need to get over this ridiculous fixation you have with actually leaving when you plan to leave. After all, what is time, anyway? I don't have a good answer, but we sure as hell know when we're not on it. And that's the crux of the problem. Time itself is an abstract concept, your wife is not. So just let go of regular time, and embrace "wife time." The central tautology of "wife time" is this: You will leave when she is ready, and she'll be ready when she's ready (and then you'll leave). Seems simple enough, and yet most men seem to have great difficulty grasping the inherent truth of it. Luckily, there is help for you.

You may entertain the notion of just learning to be late yourself. That way, you'll spend less time waiting for her, right? Bad idea. Think about it: Whenever she makes you late and you acknowledge that fact, it somehow becomes your fault in the end. Imagine if it actually was your fault. You'd end up the recipient of some mutant, apology-resistant form of blame, immune to all known forms of husbandly ass-kissing.

One thing you could try is using what our friends in the psychotherapy community refer to as "affirmations." The idea is that you can recondition your brain by just telling yourself over and over again that you are a relaxed and patient sweetheart rather than a frustrated, impatient psychopath. You'll want to come up with two or three affirmations, and make them positive statements in the present tense.

So every day take a few minutes and repeat the following affirmations ten times: "I am patient. I'm comfortable being late. I'm happy to wait until she's ready to leave." Over time, you may actually become the type of person that your affirmations describe.

If that doesn't work, you can always rely on your good friend television. But be careful, you don't want to get started with anything you can't easily turn off. If you get caught up in a sporting event, you risk having to watch just one more play, and thus taking the blame for being late (see "mutant, apology-resistant blame," above). What you want to do is have an all-time favorite tape or DVD on hand, one that you can watch for ten minutes at any point, be totally entertained, and then turn off as soon as you hear the final flush and footsteps on the stairs. For me, it's *The Big Lebowski, This Is Spinal Tap,* or *Dr. Strangelove.* Television shows are also great, like *The Simpsons, M*A*S*H,* or *South Park.*

If that doesn't work either, and you're still consumed by her prolonged and inexplicable absence, then there's the tried and true technique of last resort: Start drinking heavily.

Finally, let's address the question of what you should do when she's finally ready to leave. You're probably thinking, "If I tell her she looks great, that's just going to reinforce the necessity of her taking so long, and I'm going to have to wait all over again next time." Or, "If I ask her what took so long, she'll probably just head back upstairs for another complete wardrobe change. It's like I'm married to freaking Cher." There must be something you can say that will both make her feel good and get her to spend less time getting ready in the future. Nope, there isn't. Just tell her she looks great and then keep your big mouth shut.

How to Ask for Directions

There are countless theories about why men won't ask for directions—they're too insecure to admit failure, too stubborn to ask for help, or they just love the challenge—but here's one that seems right on the mark, and I'm sure most men will agree. University of Pittsburgh anthropologist Steve Gaulin tested how quickly two different species of male voles (a hamsterlike rodent) learned to navigate a maze. One type, the meadow vole, is a polygamous drifter, traveling great distances in a constant search for new romantic conquests. The other type, the pine vole, is monogamous and stays close to home. Gaulin's study found that male meadow voles learned new mazes more quickly than male pine voles or females of either species.

So, the real answer to the question "Why won't men ask for directions?" is simply that you can always find a Hooter's when you really need one. Given that unfortunate reality, we still need to come up with a plan to help men placate their wives' desperate need to ask for directions.

Let's face it, the truth is (as the aforementioned study confirms) that at the time women start badgering their husbands to stop and ask for directions, he's just not yet lost. And all that nagging is interfering with his fine-tuned navigational instincts (Dr. Gaulin should set it up so Mrs. Meadow Vole rides shotgun through the maze, and then we'll see how well the male vole does), so when they actually do become lost, it's really her fault. But this is all about becoming the perfect husband, and the road to perfection is definitely not best traveled by telling her the truth. So as we all well know, when the truth won't work, avoidance usually will.

Print Out Online Directions

Go to Yahoo Maps or MapQuest and print out the directions to your destination. Make a big display of handing her the papers, and say something like "Your charts, Ms. Navigator." Then, when you get lost, either the directions were wrong or she screwed up. She'll have to get out and ask the guy at the gas station, and you can sit there free from blame. Or course, if you pass by the local Hooter's, you may want to volunteer to run in and get help yourself.

Get a GPS

Global Positioning Systems use satellites to plot your exact location, sometimes within a range of just a few inches. This is one of those rare gadgets that she wants you to have as much as you want to have it. Driving with a GPS means never having to say "We're lost," and consequently never having to ask for directions. Problem solved. Let's just hope they never figure out a way to use your wife's voice for the audio guidance.

How to Appear Calm While She's Driving

Let's face it, digging your nails into the dashboard every time she takes the wheel is bad for your blood pressure and your car's resale value. You've got a few different options here: If you focus on the random stops, the distracted swerving, and every nearly missed turn, you'll only make her more nervous, and you'll invariably be blamed for any and all blunders. So your best bet is to remain calm, or at least create the illusion of calmness.

To achieve this trancelike state, we will rely on the wisdom of the Buddhist monks, whose practices of observational breathing and visualization have helped husbands remain calm while riding shotgun for thousands of years.

Assume the Position

After she comes out of that hairpin turn and you can dislodge your trachea from the shoulder strap, rest your feet flat on the floor and place your hands comfortably on your lap or on your legs. Sit up straight, with your head tilted slightly forward (so you're looking down at the reassuring vision of the passenger-side airbag).

Follow Your Breathing

Breathe normally through your nose, and focus on the breath as it enters your nose and flows down into your lungs. Imagine

you're breathing in calmness and relaxation. As you exhale out your mouth, imagine that the sheer terror (and your impulse to make final peace with Jesus) exits your body with each out-breath.

Visualization

After you are able to focus on your breath to the exclusion of the high-speed mayhem going on just a thin, plate-glass thickness from your head, you can try to further immerse yourself in meditation. Imagine yourself floating in a few feet of perfectly warm water, the sun on your face, with the waves gently rolling in on the rhythm of your breathing.

If the car's Joe Cocker–like gyrations make it impossible to follow your breathing, try this method: Tense up all the muscles in your left foot as tight as you can. Concentrate on the tension and focus solely on that feeling. Then, release the muscles and concentrate on the sense of relaxation you feel in that area. Repeat with your other foot, then move all around your body, tensing and relaxing. One of the best is tightening your whole face, then releasing. It's fun, and you just know it looks ridiculous, but make sure she doesn't see you doing it or she'll think you're having a stress-induced stroke.

How to Pretend Not to Look at Other Women

Difficulty
T T
Reward
♥ ♥ ♥

"Get a good look, Costanza?!"
—NBC President Russell Dalrymple,
to George, on "Seinfeld"

Getting caught sucks. You know the scenario: You're walking down the street arm in arm with your wife, wedding bands a-glimmerin' in the midday sun, and you get nabbed ogling some hot young chick in a belly shirt who is more likely to mistake you for Dennis Franz than join you for a steamy weekend in Barbados. Your wife thinks you're an idiot, the hot chick thinks you're, like, Mick Jagger–old (and married!), and you're literally left holding the bag as your wife drags you along for an afternoon of grudge shopping. Like I said, getting caught sucks. So don't get caught.

The art of the covert gawk is just that, an art. I can offer a few strategies to better your chances of success, but keep in mind that each man brings his own special abilities to the table. So utilize these strategies to the extent that they work for you, but feel free to make alterations to suit your own unique tastes and talents. Regardless of your approach, remember that Jerry Seinfeld was correct: Checking out a chick is like looking into the sun. You can't just stop and stare, you've got to get a quick peek and then look away fast.

You Gotta Wear Shades

Dark or mirrored sunglasses are obviously the traditional tools of the trade. They do present a few problems, though. First of all, the darker the shades, the less of a view you're going to get. This is an issue for the peeping purist. Second, and more problematic, is that sunglasses can make you careless. You figure your glasses give you a free rein to scope out the scenery, and you forget that just before you noticed that fabulous babe you were carrying on a conversation with your wife. Suddenly, complete tunnel vision sets in and you go stone-cold silent. Only tripping over your tongue would be more obvious. And if you're wearing mirrored glasses, remember that if the subject of your gaze can see herself, she knows you can, too. Glasses can provide some cover, but you've still got to put in the effort of pretending you're not looking.

The Body Scan

You're walking down the street with your wife, and you notice a fine young lady approaching. You can't just drop everything and whip out the opera glasses. Realize that you'll only get a quick glimpse, and that has to be enough. You want to get the best view possible without incurring the wrath of either woman. What you want to do is keep walking, looking down at the ground in front of you. If you're talking with your wife, maintain a normal conversational cadence. As you sense the subject approaching, do a smooth, steady scan of her from toe to head. Don't stop along the way to browse, or you're dead meat. This move gives the impression of coincidence; you're just raising your head to keep your eyes forward and avoid bumping into other pedestrians. If your eyes meet, just give a quick, friendly nod and then move your glance straight ahead. No harm, no foul.

The Ricochet

I don't know about you, but as soon as I see someone worth getting a good, long look at, I immediately look for indirect lines of sight. If I'm driving, the passenger-side mirror is great for pedestrians. Downtown, use reflective shop windows to look back over your shoulder. The possibilities are limitless, so just be creative and utilize whatever resources are available.

The Tactical Retreat

If you do get caught, there are a few things you can do to mitigate the consequences. Realize that your wife probably notices different, less bodacious attributes of other women than you do. Tell your wife that you noticed the other woman's earrings or eyebrows, or that you thought her blouse was a really interesting color. If it's just too obvious what you were up to, if the other woman has enormous . . . uh . . . how can I say this delicately . . . hooters, say something like, "I think I know what she got for Christmas." The only thing your wife thinks is more ridiculous than fake boobs and Daisy Dukes is your obsession with them. A good joke about them will make her think you're not nearly as big a moron as you actually are.

Finally, if all else fails, you do have one final strategy to let you enjoy the scenery with a minimum of risk: Become an ass man.

How to Defend Her Honor

"First, you gotta scream like a woman and keep sobbing until the other guy turns away in disgust. That's when it's time to kick some back! And then when he's lying on the ground, kick him in the rib, step on his neck, and run like hell."

—HOMER SIMPSON

You're out together at a bar somewhere, and some jackass is giving your wife a hard time. Maybe he hits on her, and then insults her when she turns him down. You'll shoot him your best badass glare, and she'll turn to you and say something like, "Honey, just ignore him and let's get out of here." But, no matter how mature and conciliatory she may seem on the surface, deep down inside, a part of her wants you to beat the living crap out of this guy.

You may be thinking, "How can I lose?" (in which case, see "How to Know Your Limitations," page 7). If you follow her lead and walk away, you're the mature, reserved gentleman. If you fight and win, you're her rugged, dangerous hero. If you fight and lose, then it's "Oh, you poor baby" and lots of tender kisses on the cheek until the swelling goes down and you can see through both eyes again. In reality, this situation can get very ugly very quickly, and the consequences can be serious. So you've got to know how to handle things, and fast.

Walking away should always be your first option, particularly when you're in an unfamiliar place, or any time the other guy has that look in his eye like he could kick your ass quite handily without leaving his seat or spilling his drink. In fact, it's your legal obligation to leave, unless there's no way out and you're in immediate danger of bodily harm. So what happens if you have to stand your ground, and this guy won't back off?

Sammy Franco is one of the world's foremost authorities on both armed and unarmed combat, an innovator in "reality-based self-defense," and a guy who does not lose fights. But even he stresses the importance of de-escalating the situation before it turns violent. "Don't start giving the guy commands, not even things like 'calm down' or 'relax,' " Franco says, "but take a hit to your ego and use choice words like 'excuse me' or 'oops, my fault.' " Also, use nonverbal cues to calm the situation. Franco recommends creating some space between you and the other guy (at least five feet) and spreading your arms slightly with your palms up in a nonthreatening pose. The space will give you greater reaction time, and the pose accomplishes several things: Not only does it de-escalate the situation, but it also tells witnesses and bouncers that you are not the aggressor. Finally, it puts you in a good position to strike if you're forced to (see below).

You don't want to make things worse by clenching your fists or pointing a finger at the guy, what Franco calls "the parental finger (you know, the Dikembe Mutombo move)." He also suggests you look for cues that the other guy is about to lose it, such as his face going dark red, rapid and incoherent speech, stuttering or yelling, clenched fists and tense shoulders, or what police call the "thousand-yard stare," when he just stares right through you. Also, notice if he looks around to the left and right, checking for witnesses before he goes off.

If he gets in your space (within what Franco calls "bad breath range"), stand up without threatening him, and make sure your wife has a clear exit route and that she takes it. Don't go pointing a finger at the guy or push him away. That makes you the aggressor. Remain in your de-escalation pose with your palms up.

If your gut is telling you this guy is going to swing at you, or you notice him "chambering a punch" by cocking his arm back, make sure you hit him first. Franco recommends you hit him with a "palm-heel strike" to the chin. From your de-escalation pose, just turn with your dominant side and strike upward with the butt of your palm to his chin.

Another strike you can try is called the "short arc hammer fist." This time you make a fist and smash down on the bridge of his nose with the meaty part of your hand (on the pinkie side). He won't see it coming, and afterward his vision will be

seriously impaired once those tear ducts get going. "Also," Franco notes, "his nose is going to explode, so that'll be the end of your shirt, since it'll just be covered in blood."

Finally, if you don't strike quickly enough, Franco has some tips to help you defend against a punch. First, as you're trying to de-escalate, notice which hand he's drinking with. That will probably be his dominant hand (also, his watch will probably be on his off hand). The most common punch in the United States is the right-hand haymaker, a curving punch directed at the left side of your head (oddly enough, Franco notes, in Ireland the most common attack is a head butt). Franco suggests you use a right hand mid-block to defend against this. Bring your left arm out in front of you, bent a bit more than ninety degrees. Turn your forearm away from you and bring your arm up and out to block his punch with the "belly" of your forearm, the meaty part between the wrist and elbow. This move should deflect his punch, and leave him open for a palm-heel strike or a short-arc hammer fist with your right hand.

And when it's all over, "get the hell outta there," Franco warns. "You don't want to be around if this guy comes looking for you with his buddies, or a gun."

Here are a few other tips from Franco:

1. If things are getting uncomfortable, try just switching seats with her.
2. Don't drink too much.
3. Befriend the bouncers (acknowledge their tough job; give a tip).
4. Never kick in a bar fight. There's no room, the floor could be slippery, and so on.
5. Be sure your wife knows not to get involved, to just leave if things get rough.

Sammy Franco is the founder and creator of Contemporary Fighting Arts (CFA), a scientific and practical combat system designed specifically to provide the most efficient, effective, and safe methods possible to avoid, defuse, confront, and neutralize both armed and unarmed assailants. Mr. Franco is also a law-enforcement master instructor and the author of nine best-selling books on street self-defense. For more information, visit his website: www.sammyfranco.com.

How to Play a Round of Golf in Two Hours

If watching Sergio Garcia play golf doesn't send you into furious fits of rage, lobbing a half-full beer at the television with each plaintive cry of "Just hit the freaking ball already," then you're in big trouble in this department. Face it, now that you're married you just can't disappear for five or six hours on a Saturday, return home exhausted and stinking of beer and goose crap, and expect a warm reception from the wife. But giving up golf altogether is just not an option. So, here are ten simple tricks to help you get on and off the links as quickly as possible.

1. *Get out early.* Find out when the course opens, and get that first tee time. Nothing guarantees a quick round like being the first on the course, and there's a chance you'll get home before she's even awake.

2. *Play in the rain.* I used to love playing in the rain. The course empties out, the greens soften up, and everything within six feet becomes a gimme since everyone in your group just wants to get the hell off the course. Just remember, when the thunderstorms roll in, you should avoid swinging those lightning rods around your torso (especially the Big Bertha).

3. *Get a like-minded foursome together.* It only takes one guy to kill a speed round. The worst is the oblivious hack, the guy who takes several practice swings and stands over the ball for five minutes before launching a worm-burner into the trees. Make sure everyone in your group is on the same page.

4. *No practice swings.* How many times have you taken three perfect practice swings, and then when you swing for real you send a mattress-sized divot twirling down the fairway? Warm up with a few swings before your round, and that's it. Practice swings are what driving ranges are for. And face it, putting is just blind luck, so all the practice strokes in the world won't help you there.

5. *Bring your "foot wedge" and "hand wedge."* Face it, you're never going pro, but you'd still like to beat your buddies. Why risk losing two or three strokes in the trap or because you're behind a tree? Just kick the ball clear when nobody's looking. If you're in a deep bunker where nobody can see you, pick the ball up and hold it in your right hand while you take a big swing. Just as you kick up a huge torrent of sand, toss the ball over your head and onto the green. Nice shot, Tiger.

6. *Leave lost balls.* Unless you can spot the ball from the edge of the tree line, or within reach of the shore, it's gone. If the ball is obviously lost, take the penalty stroke. If there's the slightest chance you could've found it, walk behind a tree and drop a new one covertly (see #5).

7. *Learn the art of playing through.* This one is a little tricky, and should only be utilized when it's clear that you're playing much faster than the people ahead of you and there are clear fairways ahead of them. You don't want to just hit into them, and it's hard to ask nicely when you're screaming from the tee box. If there's a sharp turn in the course, so you're walking close by as they head down the next fairway, tell the group in front of you that your wife will kill you if you're not home by lunchtime, and would they mind if you played through at the next par 3. Or, just skip ahead to the next tee when they're hitting their approach shots (and yes, you would've sunk a twenty-foot birdie putt on the green you skipped, so just give yourself the birdie).

If you do happen to encounter unreasonable resistance to your playing through, here's a good way to piss them off. When they're putting on a par 3, stand on the tee box like you're about to hit, but without a ball on the tee. Synchronize your fake swing with another guy in your group, who actually hits a ball safely into the woods at the same time. Then just yell, "Fore on the green!" and watch them scatter. It's funnier if you're drunk.

8. *Don't stop at the turn.* Time moves at a completely different pace within the clubhouse than on the course. It's like stopping for lunch at a highway rest stop. Before you know it, an hour has passed and you've still got half a hot dog and two Grandma's Choco-Chip Cookies to eat. To avoid this time suck, just bring snacks with you and eat on the course.

9. *Clean up your game.* The better you play, the faster you play. Take something off your swing and just go for accuracy. Shorten your backswing, and leave the driver in the bag. And even if your accuracy doesn't improve, you won't have to trek as deep into the woods to get to your ball.

10. *Play with clients during the week.* This isn't really a tip for playing faster, but if you cut out of work early, who gives a crap how long you're out there? Plus, you can get them to pick up the tab. I would suggest you not push your luck—forgo that fifth round of beers in the clubhouse before you head home. Dinner's waiting.

How to Act Like You Know Wine

The world of wine can seem overwhelming and intimidating. There's so much to learn that it seems impossible to know where to begin. For our crash course in enology (that's "the study of wine and wine making") we're going to narrow our focus down to two basic questions: What should I drink, and how should I drink it?

What Wines Should I Drink?

There is only one hard and fast rule that should govern all your wine consumption: Drink what you like. Don't worry about "red wine with meat, white with fish (or white meat)" and all the snooty sommeliers who snort with disdain when you order otherwise. Sure, there are plenty of guidelines to help you pair wines with food, but the ultimate arbiter is your own personal preference. Unfortunately, figuring out what you like may be more difficult than you'd think. The good news is that doing so requires lots and lots of drinking. So, let's get started.

There's a very useful irony in the world of wine: To look like you've got all the answers, ask a lot of questions. Since the universe of wine knowledge is infinite, everyone is pretty much in the same boat. Asking questions is not the mark of ignorance, but of the inquiring mind of an emerging connoisseur. And the simplest and most effective question of all is, "What would you recommend?" Whether you're at the liquor store on the corner or the fancy French restaurant downtown, tell them what's for dinner and ask for suggestions. It also helps to give a price range. If you're not sure about price, just tell them you want a good value. They'll suggest wines from a few different price ranges, and you can decide. Then, the next time you're in that situation, just mention the previous wine, tell them whether you liked it or not, and ask for more help. Before you know it, you'll be a big fan of Spanish reds, or you'll hate Chardonnays. Whatever, it's all up to you. And the more you know, the more you'll want to know, and the easier it will become to keep learning.

Tips for developing your taste in wine:

1. Go to wine tastings at vineyards, try many different wines, and ask lots of questions.

2. Go to restaurants that offer tasting menus that match wines with food. Pay attention to how the wines complement the food.

3. Ask your friends to recommend wines they like.

How Do I Drink Wine?

Drinking wine may seem like a minefield of potentially embarrassing rituals, but it's really not that complicated. When you're out at a restaurant, and it comes time to select the wine, follow the suggestions above. The waiter or sommelier (any restaurant with wines on the list for more than $25 should have someone around who knows wine) will present the bottle for you to inspect to make sure it's the one you requested. If you've already forgotten what you ordered, just nod and smile. He will then uncork the bottle, pour an ounce or two, and present it to you. You do not need to sniff the cork at this point, but you should check to see that it's not dried out and brittle. When you receive your glass, give it a quick swirl to release the aroma of the wine, take a deep sniff, then knock it back. You're checking to see if the wine is "corked," if it has been spoiled by a mold that can exist in improperly prepared corks. Corked wine smells like moldy newspapers, and should be rejected. If the wine doesn't taste right to you, but you're not sure it's corked, you can ask the sommelier for a second opinion. If the wine tastes fine, simply acknowledge that and you're all set.

When serving wine at home, there are several other things you need to know. First, the temperature of the wine is very important. Red wines should be served just a bit below room temperature, and white wines should be rather cool, but not ice cold. You shouldn't store any wine in the refrigerator for long periods of time, but merely chill them as necessary just before serving.

There are many different types of wine glasses, but you only need to have two. White wine glasses are the standard, tulip-shaped glasses. Red wine glasses have a larger, more rounded bowl. The glasses are designed to accentuate the particular aromas of the wine and focus the pour of the wine on the particular taste buds central to enjoying each wine. If you drink champagne or other sparkling wines, you might also want to have champagne flutes on hand. The narrow bowl of the flute is designed to preserve the carbonation of the champagne as long as possible. When drinking white or sparkling wines, you'll always want to hold the glass by the stem, rather than the bowl. That way, the heat from your hand won't warm the wine.

You've got countless corkscrew options these days, but the classic will always be the simple corkscrew, or "wine key" (you know, the one with the corkscrew that flips out, the metal tab, and the little knife blade). There's nothing cooler than a quick, smooth opening of a bottle with a wine key. It's actually quite simple:

1. Use the knife blade to cut the foil off the top of the bottle. While most people will cut the foil at the very top of the bottle, you're actually supposed to cut it off below the thickened lip at the top.

2. Hold the corkscrew perpendicular to the cork, with the tip of the screw pointing down into the center of the cork. In a single motion, press the tip down into the cork, twist the corkscrew to further set the screw and bring it up so it's pointing straight down into the cork.

3. Twist the corkscrew until the entire coil is inside the cork.

4. Raise the metal tab of the corkscrew until the notched edge is resting on the lip of the bottle. Hold it firmly in place with your off hand.

5. Pull up on the lever of the corkscrew slowly until the cork is removed, then wipe the lip of the bottle clean with a towel.

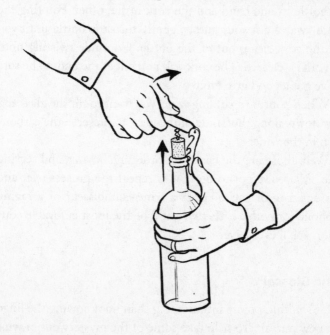

When pouring wine for your guests, you want to pour into the center of the glass and fill the glasses about two-thirds full. At the end of each pour, give the bottle a quick quarter-turn while lifting the bottle to catch any drips. It is also completely acceptable to wipe the bottle clean with a towel after each pour.

We've all seen champagne bottles shaken up and opened with a furious blast and a cork shot across the room. With the exception of certain New Year's Eve parties and America's Cup victories, you'll want to take a more subdued approach to opening your sparkling wine.

1. Unwrap the foil from atop the cork, and then untwist the wire at the base of the cork. If the cork starts rising out of the bottle, hold it firmly and let it rise up out of the bottle very slowly.

2. Remove the wire covering and discard. Hold the base of the bottle in one hand and the cork in the other. Pointing the bottle away from your guests, gently turn the bottle until you feel the cork rising out of the bottle. Continue twisting until the cork is released. The cork will pop out at the end, so be sure you've got a good grip on it.

When pouring sparkling wine, you want to tilt the glass and pour down along the inside of the glass to preserve the carbonation in the wine.

Well, those are the basics for ordering, buying, and serving wine. All you've got to do now is repeat the process over and over again until you're either a wine connoisseur or a raging alcoholic (or both). Either way, it'll be the most enjoyable education you'll ever have.

Wine Glossary

There's nothing more intimidating than not knowing the lingo of a new pursuit. To help take some of the mystery out of wine and wine tasting, here are a few of the more commonly used terms.

Appellation: A designated growing region, from which a wine gets its name. Appellations are tightly regulated to preserve the unique qualities of the wines produced there. For example, Burgundy, Bordeaux, and Champagne are all wine producing regions in France, and wines produced there must meet the set standards to bear the name.

Balance: A harmony achieved among the components of the wine—the tannins, fruitiness, acidity, and alcohol. The specifics may not mean anything to you at first, but over time you'll come to appreciate a well-balanced wine.

Body: The sense of the wine's fullness or weight in the mouth, or its richness and lingering flavor. Wines are described as full-, light-, or medium-bodied. Some wines, like champagnes, are meant to be light-bodied.

Bouquet: The complex fragrance of a wine that develops as it ages. In contrast, "aroma" usually just means the smell of grapes, which is very prominent in young wines, and "nose" is just a simple assessment of the smell of the wine.

Corked: This does not mean that you've hacked up the cork and there are bits of if floating in the wine. It refers to a spoiled wine that has a strong moldy smell and taste due to exposure to a chemical compound (TCA) from a faulty cork.

Dry: A wine in which most or all of the sugar in the grapes has fermented to alcohol, as opposed to sweet wines in which more residual sugar remains. Acids in the wine can also give a sense of dryness, masking the sugar that it may contain. Keep in mind that dry wines can be very fruity, and give the impression of sweetness even though they're very low in residual sugar.

Finish: The aftertaste and lingering aroma of a wine. A good wine should have a long, smooth finish.

Legs: The viscous streams of wine that cling to the sides of a glass after it has been swirled. Lingering legs indicate richness and full body.

Sweet: A wine with high sugar content, either residual sugar left after the fermentation process was stopped, or sugar that was added during fermentation.

Tannins: Chemical compounds that come from the skins and seeds of grapes and other fruits (and even tree bark) and are crucial to wine making. They are more prominent in red wine than white, and can give wines an astringent or puckering quality. It's usually the tannin levels in red wine that give some people headaches.

Varietal: A wine named for the grapes used to make it, such as Merlot, Cabernet, or Chardonnay. Most American wines are named this way.

How to Fix a Flat Tire

When was the last time you checked your tire pressure? Probably can't remember, can you? How about the last time you checked the pressure on your spare tire? Or even checked to see that you actually have a spare? The first rule of tire changing is: Do everything you can to never have to change a tire, and that means checking your tire pressure at least once a month. Check the sides of your tires for the correct pressure specifications, and be careful not to overinflate. While you're at it, check for any irregularities like asymmetric wear of the tread or bubbling on the sidewalls. Also check to make sure your treads aren't too worn down. One easy method for this is called the "penny test." When you place a penny in between the tire treads, you shouldn't be able to see Lincoln's head. If you can, it's time for new tires.

The second rule is: Be prepared just in case. That means having everything you need if you get a flat. First, make sure your AAA membership is up to date and your cell phone is charged. Next, check to see that you've actually got a spare tire in the trunk and that it's properly inflated. Make sure you've got a jack and a tire iron (they should be either under the spare or in a little compartment nearby), and you may want to throw a can of WD-40 in there as well in case the lug nuts stick on you.

So, you're driving along just fine, when suddenly the car starts to rattle and shake, and the steering wheel is jerking around on you. The first thing you have to do is get the car safely off the road. That means putting on your hazards and moving the car onto a flat surface as far off the roadway as possible.

Remember, the perfect husband doesn't need to constantly prove his manhood. He can delegate and call in experts when necessary. So, use that charged-up cell phone to call AAA. This should always be your first plan of attack.

But suppose you're out in the middle of nowhere, you've got no cell phone reception, and you're stuck with a flat tire. You're on your own, and you've got no choice but to take matters into your own hands.

First, make sure your hazards are on and engage the parking brake. If you've got any flares in your car, light them and position them behind your car about thirty feet apart. Next, get out the tire iron or lug wrench (you may have a single tool that acts as both, and doubles as the jack handle), jack, and spare tire. With the car still on the ground, pry off the hubcap with the tire iron. Then loosen the lug nuts. This may be easier said than done, so if they won't loosen, try spraying with a little WD-40 and let it penetrate for a few minutes. If that still doesn't do the trick, try stepping down hard on the lug wrench (remember "lefty loosey," which means you step on the side to the left). Loosen the first nut, then loosen the one directly across from it. Make your way around until all the lug nuts are loose, leaving them still threaded on the bolts.

If you've never jacked up your car before, this is a good time to refer to the owner's manual (actually, anytime before the blowout was a better time, but this time will have to do). Remember what we talked about in "How to Know Your Limitations" (page 7)? Well, this is one of those times when the potential consequences of screwing up are too severe not to educate yourself fully before getting started. The two most important things the manual will tell you are where to place the jack and how to safely release the jack and lower the car. Make sure you understand these two points before beginning.

Jack up the car until the flat tire is off the ground. Now remove the lug nuts and keep them all together someplace (if you've got hubcaps, place them in the one that you removed). Take off the flat tire and replace it with the spare, making sure the air valve is facing out. Now, put the lug nuts back on, just tightening them by hand, following the same pattern you used to loosen them (first one nut, then the one directly across from it, and so on around the tire).

Carefully release the jack (recheck the owner's manual if you didn't read these instructions carefully the first time, and I'm assuming you didn't) and lower the car fully. Now, tighten the bolts as hard as you possibly can. Put the flat tire and your tools in the trunk, and don't forget the flares. That's it, you're done.

Keep in mind that a spare tire is not meant to be driven fast or for any great distance. Get to a service station as quickly as possible to see if your old tire can be fixed, or if it needs to be replaced.

And as soon as you get home try to find a cell phone service that has better freaking coverage.

How to Tie a Bow Tie

Difficulty
T T T T
Reward
♥ ♥ ♥ ♥

I'm assuming you can dress yourself in a regular suit and tie, otherwise you'd never have found anybody to marry you in the first place. But one mystery that continues to elude even the most assiduously married among us is how to tie a real bow tie.

When I was a kid, my mother used to tell the orthodontist that she didn't want my teeth to look too perfect (I believe she used the term "Osmondesque"). It's the same with bow ties. Clip-ons look too perfect. There's something brilliantly rakish about the slightly asymmetric, curiously crumpled look of a real bow tie. And best of all, when the night is through, there's nothing classier, nothing more perfectly Sinatra-like than sipping a cool scotch on the rocks with an untied bow tie slung around your collar. With a clip-on, the best you can hope for is Kent Dorfman and warm beer dregs.

Keep in mind that tying a bow tie takes lots of practice. Be patient, follow these instructions, and you'll be looking groovy in no time, baby.

Step 1

Mix yourself a strong drink (see "How to Become a Martini Guy," page 149). You're gonna need it.

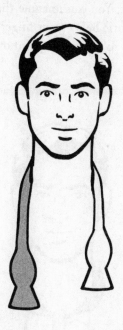

Step 2

Hang the bow tie around your neck, with the right side about an inch lower. These instructions assume that you're right-handed. If you're left-handed, just switch everything around.

Step 3

Bring the longer end across and over the shorter end, tuck it up through the hole, pull it snug around your neck, then toss the left side up onto your left shoulder (the underside of the tie should be showing).

Step 4

With your right hand, grasp the flap on the right where it narrows near the end (index finger on the front, thumb behind). That point will be the middle of the tie. You can imagine the width of the tie will be the length of fabric below your fingers plus an equal length above (pretty much to the fattest point on the fabric above your fingers).

Step 5

Holding the tie pointing straight down, turn it counterclockwise to horizontal and press it up against your neck with your thumbnail right against the first knot you made. Remove your thumb from underneath, and hold that flap there with your index finger pressing against the middle of the tie onto the knot underneath. You should have a loose end sticking out to the right and a looped end to the left.

Step 6

Grab the flap on your shoulder with your left hand and drape it over the first flap so it's pointing straight down. Hold everything in place with your right index finger. Now pinch the two flaps together in front between your right thumb and middle finger, with the vertical flap sticking down in between.

Step 7

Grasp the vertical flap with your left thumb and index finger, at the thickest point above the narrowing. Using your index finger as a pointer, poke that flap up behind the pinched flaps, and horizontally through the hole there from left to right.

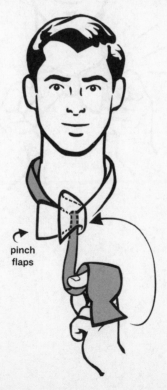

pinch
flaps

Step 8

Holding both looped ends, pull left and right to tighten the tie, and "primp" it so that both sides are even and the knot in front is clean and tight.

Now grab your dame and hit the town, mister!

How to Dance at a Wedding

Difficulty

T T

Reward

♥ ♥ ♥ ♥

The question of how you should approach the dance floor at a wedding can be answered in a single word: willingly.

To achieve this, we'll employ the "Ramius Defense." Remember in *The Hunt for Red October* when Captain Ramius turned his sub head-on into the path of that oncoming torpedo, thus forcing impact before the warhead could arm itself? Well, dancing at a wedding works the same way.

You know you're going to end up on the dance floor eventually. So save your wife the trouble of dragging you out there. Beat her to the punch and drag *her* out to the dance floor at the first opportunity. That way, you earn extra credit from the other wives at your table, who jealously watch you shake your thang, and shoot scornful glances at their own stoic, stationary spouses.

I know it's difficult, but let's see if we can help you get over your very rational fear of public jigginess.

If you've got self-image issues, just take a minute to think about who might witness your fish-flopping gyrations: Married guests sympathize completely, and your single friends think everything you do within the context of your marriage is ridiculous and embarrassing. You see, there's no real downside to dancing, and I don't need to tell you about the downside to not dancing.

Still not convinced? Still picturing yourself in the "dance of the living dead" from *Caddyshack*? Well, I've sought out my own personal "dancing guy" and asked his advice. You know the dancing guy, right? Every group of guys has one member who loves to dance. He's out there cutting loose all night, spinning any number of women around and having a great time. Ever since college, Jeff Goldberg has been our dancing guy.

CB: So, what drives you to dance?
JG: I'm not brave, talented, or an exhibitionist . . . I'm just bored! I'd rather dance than sit around and make small talk with distant relatives—or pretend I'm interested in the life story of the bride's sister's best friend's roommate. I discovered long ago that women like to do two things: dance and talk. Dancing gets me off the hook conversationally.

CB: Most guys are just too embarrassed to get out there. How do you deal with that?
JG: I get really drunk. It may not help my technique, but it eliminates inhibitions and definitely fosters creativity. Remember, dancing is just like putting and sex: Feel is more important than technique.

CB: So you don't worry about what other people think?
JG: Screw them if they can't take a joke. That's my motto and calling card. Look, the dance floor should be filled with single guys trying to hook up and married guys who don't want to sleep on the couch that night. If anyone else thinks I look ridiculous, what do I care?

CB: Finally, what about an actual dancing technique? Lots of guys just don't know what to do with themselves. Any suggestions?
JG: First of all, always try to maintain eye contact with your wife while you're dancing. Lose yourself in her eyes and that'll make it much easier to relax and loosen up. As far as how to

dance or what to do with your hands, just watch the Beastie Boys video for "Hey Ladies" and you'll be okay. (Just to be safe, you may want to go back and read "How to Know Your Limitations," page 7, before you risk spraining your groin . . . or worse.)

How to Enjoy a Chick Flick

No husband wants to look at Renée Zellweger, Gwyneth Paltrow, or Meg Ryan for ninety minutes unless they're featured in a desperate, career-salvaging spread in *Maxim*. Inevitably, of course, the wife needs a good tearjerker, and has to drag him along as punishment for something he can't remember doing (or not doing). There are ways, though, to avoid the butt-numbing misery of suffering through another interminable chick flick.

First of all, do whatever you can to convince your wife to rent the movie rather than go to the theater. Tell her you'd rather stay in, make a big bowl of popcorn, and snuggle up on the couch together. No man wants to be seen in public awaiting his own torture, let alone with the knowledge that he overpaid for the privilege.

If she demands that you go out to the theater, under no circumstances can you separate from her. Do not let her leave you alone in the ticket line or the concessions line, and most important, remain together when entering the theater. There's no more pitiful sight than a plaintive husband, extra-large popcorn tucked under his arm, calling out in search of his wife in a darkened theater.

Whether you go out or stay in, there's no rule that says you have to watch the movie the way it was meant to be watched. Here's a great way to get through any chick flick on your terms, and maybe even make a little money in the process. When I was in college, the Super Bowl was always a bit of a letdown. Since students came from all over the country, most people didn't care about either team. My friend Scott Murphy introduced us to a great Super Bowl pool that helped everyone get into the game. It consisted of true-false questions about who would win the coin toss, which beer company would have the first commercial, and whose wife would be shown first in the stands. You didn't need to know anything about football, or care about the game, to have a great time.

So why not apply Murphy's Pool to chick flicks? You know all your married friends are going to be dragged to the theater as well, so collect a few bucks from everyone, get their answers to the following questions before opening night, and it's winner take all:

The Chick Flick Pool

1. There will be a voiceover during a kiss.   T/F
2. There will be a semigraphic depiction of childbirth.   T/F
3. The villain is (or was once) married to one of the lead characters.   T/F
4. The main chick will have a phone conversation with her mother.   T/F
5. A female character will comment on the leading man's butt.   T/F
6. The chest in the obligatory naked male chest scene will be hairless.   T/F
7. The cute child who befriends the leading couple is a boy.   T/F
8. There will be a sex scene in the kitchen.   T/F
9. The main man shares his true feelings with the main chick's best friend.   T/F

10. **The soundtrack features Sheryl Crow, Avril Lavigne,
     or Dave Matthews.**   **T/F**

Feel free to add your own questions as the particular chick
flick warrants.

How to Survive the Ballet

Your wife scores tickets to the ballet, and immediately springs into action: She checks ESPN and Fox for critical conflicting events. Besides a fishing tournament, a dog show, and a new reality challenge featuring lingerie models and biker gangs, the night is all clear. And you're screwed. You're going to the ballet, like it or not (and the smart money's on "not").

You've got a few simple goals for the night: Not to make a total ass of yourself, to get it over with as quickly as possible, and to get home in time to find out who was crowned Bass Master, which bitch got best in show, and who won the Boobs vs. Bikers Bowl-a-thon. In addition, you've got to accomplish all this without falling asleep on her shoulder or whining like a jilted debutante.

Believe it or not, you can benefit from learning a bit about the ballet. Go to the ballet company's website, and print out the description of the performance you're going to see. You should actually read it, since knowing something about the performance will help it go by faster. Knowing the creators, history, and interpretation of the performance you see will increase your enjoyment of the performance as well as the pace with which it reaches its merciful conclusion. If you end up spending the evening counting the pipes in the pipe organ or trying to determine exactly how many people are in attendance, time will come to a screeching halt. So get into it a little bit.

After you've read the description of the ballet, tuck it into an outside pocket of your briefcase, making sure the header sticks out for your wife to see. That way, you'll get credit for doing your homework, and she'll think you're honestly enthusiastic about the evening's entertainment.

Don't assume you know what the appropriate attire is for the ballet. While, in theory, you can wear anything you like, in reality you have to wear what your wife tells you to wear. You know she's going to say, "A jacket and tie, of course," with a conclusive tone that implies the debate on the subject has just opened and closed within those same quotation marks. Don't fight it; just get dressed.

Once you've arrived at the theater, there will be quite a bit of milling about. At this point, your wife is extremely sensitive to any gestures or semiaudible yammerings that could embarrass her. Your best bet here is to follow her lead and say very little. Avoid words like *anorexia, bulge,* and *pratfall.* Don't mention your crush on Paula Abdul or your trip to see *Lord of the Dance* in Vegas last year.

Take a moment to skim through the program and pick the names of one or two dancers, it doesn't matter which. Otherwise, avoid reading it. You'll need every last word in there to pass the time just after the second intermission and help suppress the urge to sob plaintively until the performance concludes.

As the performance begins, try to approach it as an athletic event. You can certainly appreciate the women's bodies, and as far as the "bulge" issue is concerned, just remember that you've been able to ignore that during men's track and field events and swimming competitions, so you can ignore it here.

If you've read about the ballet, you may get some sense of what the choreographer was trying to express through the dancers. If you don't see it, don't worry. Try focusing on one dancer in particular, or even one body part. (How about trying a less obvious part of the anatomy, such as the feet or arms?) Unless you're at the New York City Ballet, odds are not all the dancers will be brilliant (there's a reason why they're in the back). Make a little game of looking for mistakes. I know it's cruel, but this is ballet and the gloves are off.

After a while, ask your wife, "Which one are you looking at?" Since most people end up focusing on one dancer, your question establishes your interest and enthusiasm. Whatever her answer, simply reply, "Yeah, she/he is really amazing."

Intermission is the time to pull out your "A" material. Remember the dancers you selected beforehand? Now's the time to use them. Say to your wife, in a voice loud enough for others around you to hear, "Boy, that Enzo Cappelletti is spectacular! What height, what extension." Or, something like, "From what I've read, that Marcus Klinghoffer seems like a direct descendent of Fernando Bujones in his early years."

When it's all over, and she asks you what you thought of the performance, simply say, "I enjoyed it more than I thought I would." If that's the truth, then good for you. If not, just pray that next time she'll get tickets to the Alvin Ailey troupe, because even you'll think they're just amazing.

How to Not Look Like a Stalker in Victoria's Secret

It's bad enough tracking your wife down in the women's department at Macy's, carefully avoiding the plus-sizes section so as not to give the impression that you're actually shopping for yourself. Finding her in Victoria's Secret presents all kinds of additional logistical problems. Yes, it is a women's store, but it's decorated like Hugh Hefner's billiard room. Part of you wants to just find your wife and leave, but another part wants to appreciate the fabulous talent on display. Let me guess which part will win out.

So you want to get some quality time in Victoria's Secret, but you'd rather not get maced or kicked in the crotch. Here are a few simple suggestions to help you enjoy the scenery and leave with the family jewels intact.

Do . . .

. . . actually walk into the store. Try to avoid standing out front, fogging up the window display with your nose pressed against the glass. (If anything else is pressed against the glass, just turn yourself in to mall security now and save them the trouble of coming to get you.)

. . . pretend to look around for your wife as soon as you walk in, bringing your left hand to your face to flash your wedding band. This will emit matrimonial vibes to the other shoppers and give you ample opportunity to check out the giant posters that adorn the walls like so many stained glass panels in this, the Church of the Righteous Booty. Can I get an *Amen?* Have mercy!

. . . ask a salesperson if your wife is in a dressing room, rather than squatting down in front of each door to see if you can recognize her by her naked ankles.

. . . sit perfectly still in the chair by the dressing room and wait for your wife to emerge. Keep your glance downward, and your hands a safe distance from your lap.

Don't . . .

. . . touch, fondle, sniff, or try on anything.

. . . giggle like a schoolgirl.

. . . use the word "panty" under any circumstances.

. . . tuck $5 bills into every mannequin's G-string.

. . . ask if they sell anything edible or crotchless.

How to Walk Slowly Through a Museum

Difficulty
T T T T
Reward
♥ ♥

I don't know about you, but for me most museum doors open some sort of portal into a parallel reality where time slows to a snail's pace, and the air and light wash over my brain like some sort of fuzzy, dull hangover. From inside looking out I see the world whizzing by, like the last scene of every *Benny Hill Show* when Benny was chasing (and then being chased by) a gaggle of scantily clad blond nurses through the park of some tony London suburb. Good times, good times.

You see, just thinking about it sets me to daydreaming. Back inside, all the other patrons seem to just float there before the artwork, completely motionless or drifting ever so slowly from room to room, turning to view each piece like the hot dogs on those rolling cookers at the 7-Eleven. To them, I must be Benny Hill, quick-stepping through the museum in a jerky blur (only without all the hot chicks in close pursuit).

None of this is ever a problem when I'm alone (although I can't remember the last time I went to a museum solo), but when I'm with my wife or other serious museumgoers, I find it's virtually impossible to slow myself down enough to stay with them. I don't want to be rude, but if we don't pick up the pace a bit my head is going to explode, and that wouldn't be terribly perfect-husband-like, now would it? So I've come up with some advice to help us take our time and enjoy the museum.

First off, the main obstacle to your appreciation of art is probably just ignorance. Imagine if you knew nothing about the nuance and lore of baseball. It would probably be a pretty boring game to watch. But once you know all the background, it becomes an intriguing drama. Go to the museum's website and read about the exhibits they currently have on display. Learning about the art and the artists will make your visit much more interesting. Just as knowing Pedro Martinez's lifetime stats can make an otherwise mundane game interesting, knowing a bit about Velázquez and his times will suddenly bring an otherwise nondescript royal portrait to life.

Next, realize that despite the Benny Hill hallucinations, time is moving at the same pace inside the museum as it is outside. Rather than letting time run away from you, try to gather it up and appreciate it while you're there. Use some of the relaxation techniques discussed earlier to focus less on the passage of time and to cultivate an inner calmness (see "How to Wait Patiently Until She's Ready to Leave," page 187; "How to Do the Dishes," page 182; and "How to Appear Calm While She's Driving," page 192).

If you can get yourself in the proper state of mind, you may find that you are suddenly more open to appreciating the art itself. And that doesn't necessarily mean liking it. Rather than reading every description of every piece and forcing yourself to find out what you think the art is supposed to be about, just clear your mind and look at it. Try to feel how the art affects you. Does it remind you of anything, or make you feel a certain way? Is it just a pretty picture? The point is, it really doesn't matter how art affects you, or if it doesn't affect you at all. Your opinion and interpretation is really the only one that matters. With this in mind, you may find yourself taking more time before each picture, just enjoying the view.

If all else fails, heed that old George Carlin edict that the best laughter is the forbidden kind, that repressed half-laugh that forces its way out at the most inappropriate moments. Museums contain limitless comic possibilities, both from the artwork and the other patrons. I remember when I was once at the Metropolitan Museum of Art in New York with my Uncle Bud and Aunt Eileen. We were standing in front of a very dark and dramatic painting of a martyred, naked woman. "What a shame," Bud said very seriously under his breath. "What?" I whispered, assuming he'd share the story of the subject's tragic demise or the artist's miserable life. Without turning away from the painting or changing the tone of his voice, he said: "Those were some great tits." A blaring, resonant snort escaped my nasal cavity, echoed all the way over to the Islamic Art gallery, and sent a huge flock of pigeons careering past the hot dog vendors on Fifth Avenue. Now that's what I call art appreciation.

How to Not Lose Too Badly in Vegas

When I was a kid, my brother and I used to go to the arcades on the boardwalk in Ocean City, New Jersey. Our parents would give us each a few dollars dollars to play Galaga, Joust, and Zaxxon at Jilly's or down at Wonderland. I'd be flat broke in about fifteen minutes, while my brother could make two dollars last two hours. I had to entertain myself, without spending any money, during the interim. Little did I know I was learning one of the most important lessons in responsible gambling: Set your budget and stick to it. Now when I go to Vegas, there's no way I will develop a gambling problem. I gamble. I lose. I hang out. No problem.

Rule #1: Set a reasonable budget, and stick to it, no matter what. To avoid temptation, leave the ATM card back in the room. Also, set your own rules for playing certain games, and stick to them. Don't suddenly get aggressive on a hunch if that's not your style. Also, since I know you're thinking about it: No, a big win the night before does not change your budget for the following night.

Of course, there's something in the air in Vegas that can mess with your head. You lose all sense of time, the free booze clouds your judgment, and you start bending the rules a little bit. You know you're in trouble when you start to think about "chasing" your losses, laying down some bigger bets to turn a losing night into a winner.

Rule #2: View gambling as entertainment. The arcade taught me another valuable lesson: I'm a loser. I'm the guy who keeps the odds securely in the house's favor. I'm no more likely to win in Vegas than I was to make money at the arcade. The odds are against you, too. So, hang out with the guys and consider your losses the cost of a good time. You wouldn't go out drinking and expect to make money on the deal, right? Same with the casino. To keep the vibe right, and your losses under control, avoid gambling alone.

Rule #3: Take frequent breaks. There's plenty of entertainment wherever you look in Vegas, so just wander along the strip and take it all in. Take an afternoon and drive out west to Red Rocks, where you can kill an entire afternoon in the natural splendor for the $5 entrance fee.

Rule #4: Appease and deceive the wife. Now, let's deal with the wife. A recent study by economist Jay Zagorsky at Ohio State University found that husbands frequently overestimate their household income, while wives often overestimate their debt. That means you've got your work cut out for you convincing your wife that dropping some major bills in Vegas is a worthwhile expenditure. So you've got two choices: Either let her set your gambling budget, or don't ever let her find out how much you lost. The former is easy to do, but hard to live with (and never let the guys find out); the latter takes a little doing, but it's worth the effort.

Squirrel away a little Vegas cash every week in your sock drawer, so even if you lose it all your wife will never know. (A friend of mine, who shall remain nameless, once hit the ATM so many times in Vegas that his wife, Mrs. Gary Lipshutz of Metuchen, New Jersey, was closed out of their account and couldn't buy lunch for herself and their baby daughter. Not good.)

You see, avoiding the big losses in Vegas is pretty easy. Just recognize that you're probably going to lose, set limits you're comfortable with, and stick to the plan. All right, since you've been such a good boy, go get yourself a lap dance or three. You've earned it.

Your Wife's Vital Stats

Here is an easy chart that you should keep on hand for future reference. Just bear in mind there's no need to actually try on her frilly underthings and footwear to confirm their sizes. Remember, "taking a walk in her shoes" is just a figure of speech.

Dress Size* _____

Shoe Size _____

Bra Size _____

Birthday _____

Reminder Holiday** _____

Anniversary _____

Reminder Holiday _____

Gift Notes: _____

_____

_____

_____

_____

_____

*If you're going to buy a dress for your wife, be absolutely sure you've got the right size for right now. Go too big, and she'll think you think she's a porker. Go too small, and she'll think you think she's a porker who needs to lose some weight. Either way, there's little room for error.
**See "How to Find the Perfect Gift" (page 55) for tips to help you remember birthdays and anniversaries.

References

Bekkar, Bruce, and Udo Wahn. *Your Guy's Guide to Gynecology: A Reference for Men and Women.* North Star Publications/Ant Hill Press, 2000.

Boyles, Denis. *A Man's Life: The Complete Instructions.* HarperPerennial, 1996.

Conrad, Barnaby. *The Martini: An Illustrated History of an American Classic.* Chronicle Books, 1995.

Courter, Gay, and Pat Gaudette. *How to Survive Your Husband's Midlife Crisis: Strategies and Stories from the Midlife Wives Club.* Perigree, 2003.

Federal Trade Commission. "All That Glitters . . . How to Buy Jewelry." *Facts for Consumers,* April 2001.

Giuffre, Kenneth. *The Care and Feeding of the Brain: How Diet and Environment Affect What You Think and Feel.* Career Press, 1999.

Gurian, Michael. *What Could He Be Thinking? How a Man's Mind Really Works.* St. Martin's Press, 2003.

Marinoff, Lou. *Plato, Not Prozac! Applying Philosophy to Everyday Problems.* HarperCollins Publishers, 1999.

Mellor, David. *Picture Perfect: Mowing Techniques for Lawns, Landscapes, and Sports.* John Wiley & Sons, 2002.

Nhat Hanh, Thich. *The Miracle of Mindfulness: A Manual on Meditation.* Beacon Press, 1987.

Roth, Dick. *"No, It's Not Hot in Here": A Husband's Guide to Understanding Menopause.* Ant Hill Press, 1999.

Schultz, Warren. *A Man's Turf: The Perfect Lawn.* Clarkson Potter, 1999.

Websites

AceFitness.org
AskMen.com
CooksIllustrated.com
LawnBoy.com
Learn2.com
MensHealth.com
RecycleNow.org
SharpMan.com

About the Author

Craig Boreth is a writer, carpenter, painter, plumber, electrician, chef, interior designer, landscape architect, mechanic, exterminator, handyman, and sharp dresser. He leaves the toilet seat down, occasionally asks for directions, and almost has six-pack abs. He lives in Santa Monica, California, with his perfect wife. Visit him at www.perfecthusband.com.